DEMOCRACY FOR YOUNG AMERICANS

by
Jerry Aten

illustrated by
Marilynn Barr

Cover by Kathryn Hyndman

ISBN No. 0-86653-483-0

Good Apple
A Division of Frank Schaffer Publications, Inc.
23740 Hawthorne Boulevard,
Torrance, CA 90505-5927

1006

Educating all citizens will enable every man to judge for himself what will secure or endanger his freedom. . . .

Thomas Jefferson

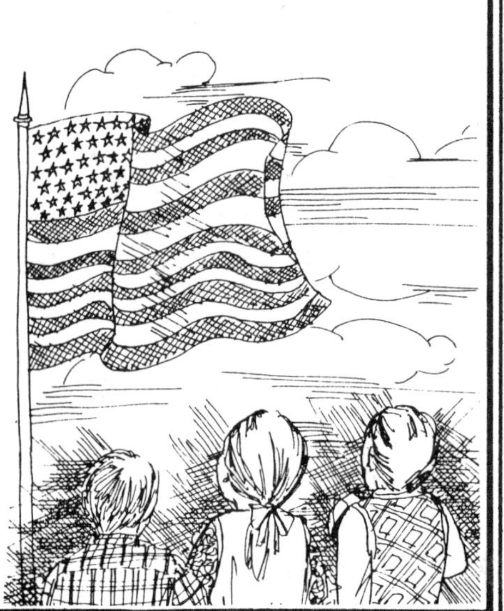

TABLE OF CONTENTS

TO THE TEACHER

One of the main tasks we as teachers are charged with is to teach our children to cherish their freedom and to accept the responsibility for preserving and passing it on to future generations. Teaching children about democracy does not mean indoctrinating them by excluding or distorting its pitfalls and shortcomings. To make our system continue to work, we need to encourage students to learn about the fundamental ideas that served as the focus for the founding fathers of this country. That focus is the magnate that holds us together as one people from a wide variety of cultures and ethnic backgrounds. Students must not only study the word, but the implications and the meanings of the Declaration of Independence, our Constitutioin and the Bill of Rights.

We should not pass on to them a body of lies. We can present our system just as it is. Presenting the truth about others, even when it shows them in a favorable light, is much better than indoctrination. If approached in a positive manner and properly done, our system will clearly stand on its own as being far superior to others. The main objective of the ideas presented in this book is to encourage our youth to do a little critical thinking and evaluating on their own of the wheels that make our system work.

We've certainly made some mistakes along the way and we will probably continue to make them in the future. Our system is not perfect and never will be. But getting children to realize the difficulties and obstacles that are encountered when the will of the people rule is what educating for democracy is all about. Other more imposing blueprints of government are indeed sometimes more efficient. But their efficiency is accomplished often at the expense of the precious freedom of the people.

There is a significant amount of values, analysis and moral education involved in teaching the concepts of democracy. But the important thing to remember is that values are not taught; rather they are encountered through experience in school and in life itself. Certain moral issues will be explored in some of the material presented in this book. But the method of their presentation will hopefully lead students to some confident conclusions about the merits of our democratic way of life. Active learning on the part of your students will occur only when you as the teacher devote adequate class time for discussion and exchanging of ideas. Many of the writing assignments get to the very heart of what students really think and feel. Let them share those ideas with others, and you will be well down the road to a democratic approach to educating children for democracy.

VOICES FROM THE CROWD

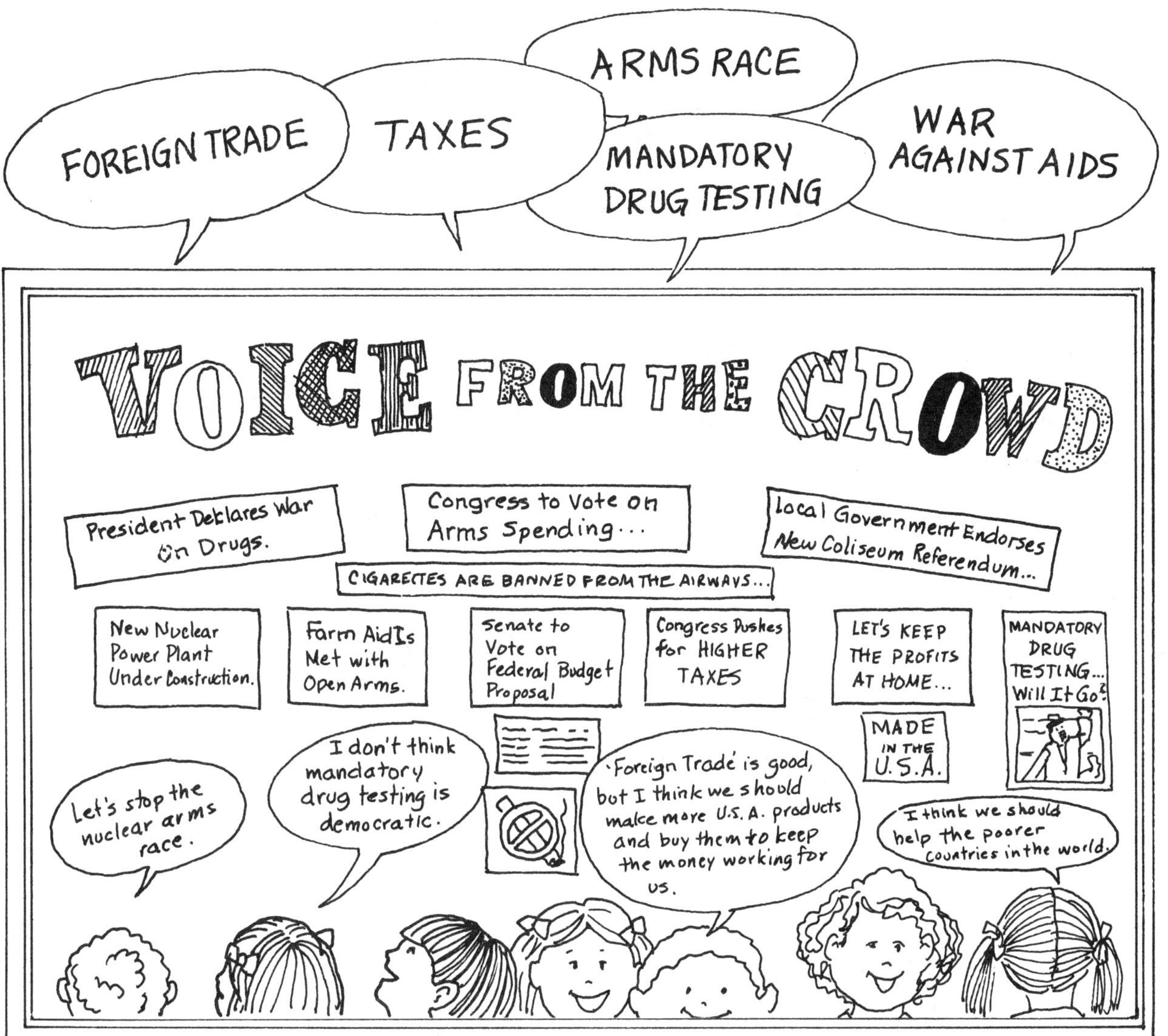

Since the real voice of democracy comes from the people themselves, it is appropriate to create a bulletin board that can be useful as well as eye-catching while studying democracy in America. First create the header for the board by making six-inch letters cut from various colors of poster board. To initiate interest on the part of the students, cut out several quotes out of context from the major news magazines (and newspapers, too, if you like) that demonstrate firm positions on issues of current importance. It's also nice to use accompanying pictures cut from the same magazines to better identify those who speak, but it isn't absolutely necessary. Encourage students to add to the board by bringing in quotes and pictures of their own choosing that suggest a firm stand on matters of topical importance. Congressmen and other politicians and leaders of specific interest groups make excellent sources for those who want to be heard. An extension of the board involves the students themselves creating "quotations" that are their own position statements as you proceed through your study of democracy.

DEMOCRACY: A MATTER OF COMMON SENSE

It was the fiery pen of Thomas Paine in his *Common Sense* that placed the power of the written word before the people during the days when revolution was still a matter of debate and consideration. Paine attempted to present the people with logical reasons why they should favor severing ties with Great Britain. One of his classic statements—"Society in every state is a blessing, but government even in its best state is but a necessary evil. . ."—perhaps sums up his philosophy best. The implication was not that we dispense with government but that we take a low and practical view of its functions.

The main purposes for having government at all, according to Paine, were to provide security against violence, to uphold the laws, to protect the property of individuals and to punish crime. The bottom line in whether or not the government should have or not have a specific power was whether or not it was useful to the people. The people would decide and restrict the powers of government to only those that really are necessary and in their best interests.

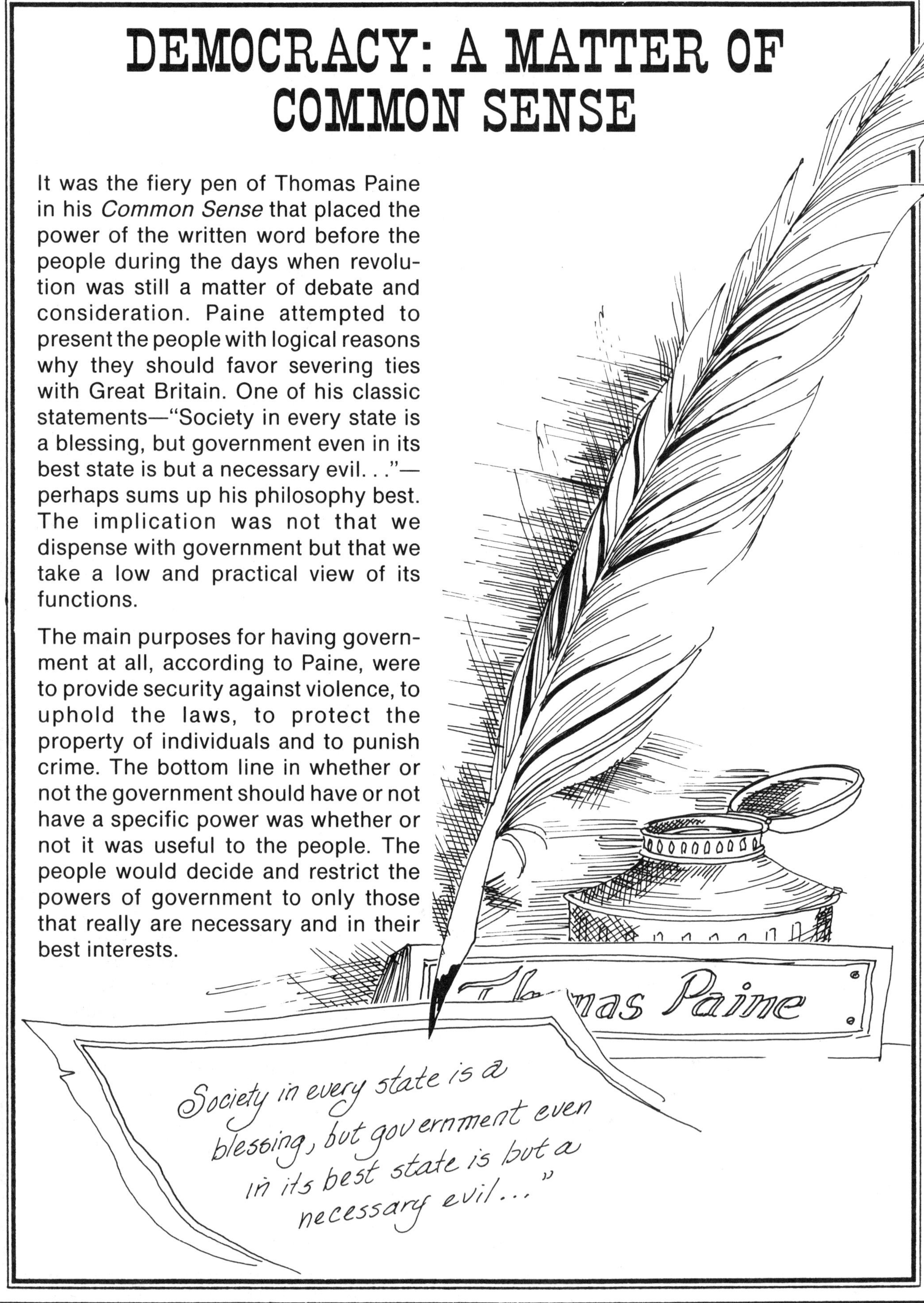
Thomas Paine
"Society in every state is a blessing, but government even in its best state is but a necessary evil..."

Name ______________________

DEMOCRACY: A MATTER OF COMMON SENSE

Thomas Paine's words did have an influence in inciting the colonists to the cause for revolution. But his reasons for government are not the only reasons that governments are not only desirable, but necessary—especially in today's society. List the reasons below why governments are not only necessary for our continued existence and survival, but also make our lives richer and fuller because of them. Share your thoughts with the rest of your class.

____

____

____

____

____

____

Can you think of any examples in our society today in which you feel the government is involved unnecessarily? If you don't feel strongly against any issue in which government is involved, jot down the single power government has today which is at least questionable.

____

____

____

____

____

____

"... but government even in its best state is but a necessary evil..."

Thomas Paine

Thomas Paine

REBELLION OR REVOLUTION

When the American colonists declared themselves free of British Parliament and the rule of King George in 1776, they really weren't trying to simply create a new society. They were making a statement about the basic rights of man and the relationship of man to his government. The fact was that British policy was threatening the very fabric of colonial life. The colonists had come to this new land seeking a fresh start. Although they had made the journey for a variety of reasons, the common thread linking those reasons was a desire for a new way of life.

Risking what little they had, the colonists arrived in this land with an almost unbridled freedom to do with their lives the best they could. Great Britain was concerned mainly with populating the colonies to protect the land from being taken over by other countries. There were few rules and regulations at first. As time passed and the colonies began to prove their worth and actually started showing a profit, things began to change. King George and Parliament began to "lend a helping hand." Rules were imposed upon them and the democratic spirit under which they had lived was taken from them.

"... and let the principles of a good government be restored and ensured for our future generations!"

By the dawn of the Revolution, it was clear to the people that the authority to rule over the people came from the people themselves. Unlike the French Revolution (and others), the American Revolution was not the work of radicals desiring to take charge. It was more a case of disposing of bad government and asserting that the principles of good government be restored and ensured for future generations. Arriving at this goal was no easy task.

Name ______________________________

REBELLION OR REVOLUTION

The Declaration of Independence was the actual vehicle used by the colonists to announce their departure from the rule of Great Britain. It was indeed a statement that formally severed the ties, but it was much more than that. The colonists systematically listed the causes leading to their decision. They cited the abuse of King George and Parliament that had taken from them the democratic way of life to which they had grown accustomed.

Obtain a copy of the Declaration and find the list of charges against Parliament and the King. After reading through the entire list, jot down the ten you feel to be the most serious violations to a democratic way of life. When your list is complete, go back through the list and rank order in terms of their importance to a democracy. (#1 will be the abuse you feel most harmful, #2 next most serious, etc.) Share your list with other members of the class. Be certain to include your reasons for the decisions you made.

ARISTOTLE'S DEMOCRACY

Over two thousand years ago Aristotle used two major criteria in classifying governments. His first was the number of persons to be served by the governing authority. His other classifications hinged upon the primary purpose toward which the governmental authority was directed. According to Aristotle, there were three different forms of government based on number—government by one, government by only a few, or government by the masses. Carrying his logic further, he then classified those subgroups according to purpose. Those purposes of government were either "true" (which would benefit all members of the governed body) or "perverted" (which would only promote the special interests of the ruling personnel).

He then refined further each of his classifications in this manner. Government by one for the benefit of all he called a *kingship* or *royalty*. If government was by one for the sole benefit of that ruler, the government was called *tyranny*. A government by the few for the benefit of all was an *aristocracy,* while government by the few for the benefit of only the special interest of those few was called an *oligarchy*. Finally, government by the many for the benefit of all was identified as a *constitutional government*, whereas government by the many for the promotion of their own selfish interests Aristotle called a *democracy*. According to Aristotle's definitions, democracy, even in its purest state, was still a perverted form of government.

Name ______________________________

ARISTOTLE'S DEMOCRACY

Why was democracy for Aristotle less than a truly good form of government?

How does our own definition of democracy differ from the way it was defined by Aristotle two thousand years ago?

LINCOLN'S DEMOCRACY

Abraham Lincoln felt that the main objective was to "elevate the condition of men. . . to afford all men an unfettered start and a fair chance in the race of life." When all the political, social, economic, geographical and moral differences between North and South eventually led them into the Civil War, the issue of slavery was not cited as being a cause. Lincoln made it his top priority to preserve the Union. He could not politically speak out against the institution of slavery. There were slave states still within the Union. There were also white men in the North who did not want to accept racial equality. But in reality Lincoln probably hoped from the start that the war would eventually bring an end to slavery. It's just that he couldn't say anything about his feelings.

As the war waged on, he began to see that a restored Union would never be the Union that was. Because of this he began to ponder thoughts of justifying an attack on slavery. His Emancipation Proclamation tied the issue of the war (restoring the Union) to the issue of slavery. From that moment on, abolition became a war aim in the eyes of most Northern people.

Once the Proclamation had been issued, there arose some question about the legality of Lincoln's executive power to make such a decision. So in the early months of 1865, Congress passed the Thirteenth Amendment, making slavery unconstitutional. The result of all this was that the Civil War was eventually used to justify a great social revolution that would make the nation a more democratic society for all.

Name ______________________

LINCOLN'S DEMOCRACY

1. Why do you think Abraham Lincoln did not support making slavery an issue the moment the Civil War broke out? Remember his belief that the main object of democracy was to give all men an equal chance in the race of life.

2. Once the Civil War had ended and the slaves had been freed, certain social problems emerged. Perhaps the greatest problem was what would now happen to the freed Blacks. In the South they had never been anything but servants. In the North they had lived under a weight of discrimination and regarded as inferior. What possibly could have been done to upgrade their status of equality once it had been declared?

3. Divide into small groups of four to five students each. Present each group with a copy of the statement below.

   "While much legislation, peaceful protest, demonstrations, bloodshed and the passing of time have all helped to bring about much improved conditions for Blacks, in America today, we all know that they still have not arrived at true equality."

   List evidence in our society that still clearly shows signs of discrimination.

   Members of the group go back through the list and record ways they feel would be most effective in eliminating such discriminations.

RIGHT VS. REWARD

There are countries on the earth whose governments distribute propaganda and make claims about being free and democratic when they aren't really either. The words *freedom* and *democracy* have a good sound to them, and they are words that people like to hear. So the political leaders of these countries dream up all kinds of fake claims that are really nothing more than words their people want to hear. But we know differently! We live in a country where we *know* what it means to be free. We *know* what democracy is all about.

Those people who live in other countries where freedom is only a word often have the definition so clouded that they confuse *reward* with *freedom*. Their confusion largely comes from their government labeling certain rewards they bestow upon people as "rights . . . and . . . freedoms to which all people are endowed . . . ."

Call them what they will, we know that nations like the Soviet Union, Communist China and Cuba are far removed from the definition of what we call a *free nation*. On the following page, you will find a list containing rights that truly can be defined as such and would exist in a free and democratic society. You will also find rewards that are disguised as rights, but which by our own notion of freedom are really nothing more than rewards. You must also realize that a government which bestows such rewards upon its people can just as easily take them away. As you go through the list on the following page, analyze each very carefully and decide which would truly fall under the definition of rights to which we all are endowed . . . and which are merely rewards. There is space beside each for you to clearly defend and explain your answer.

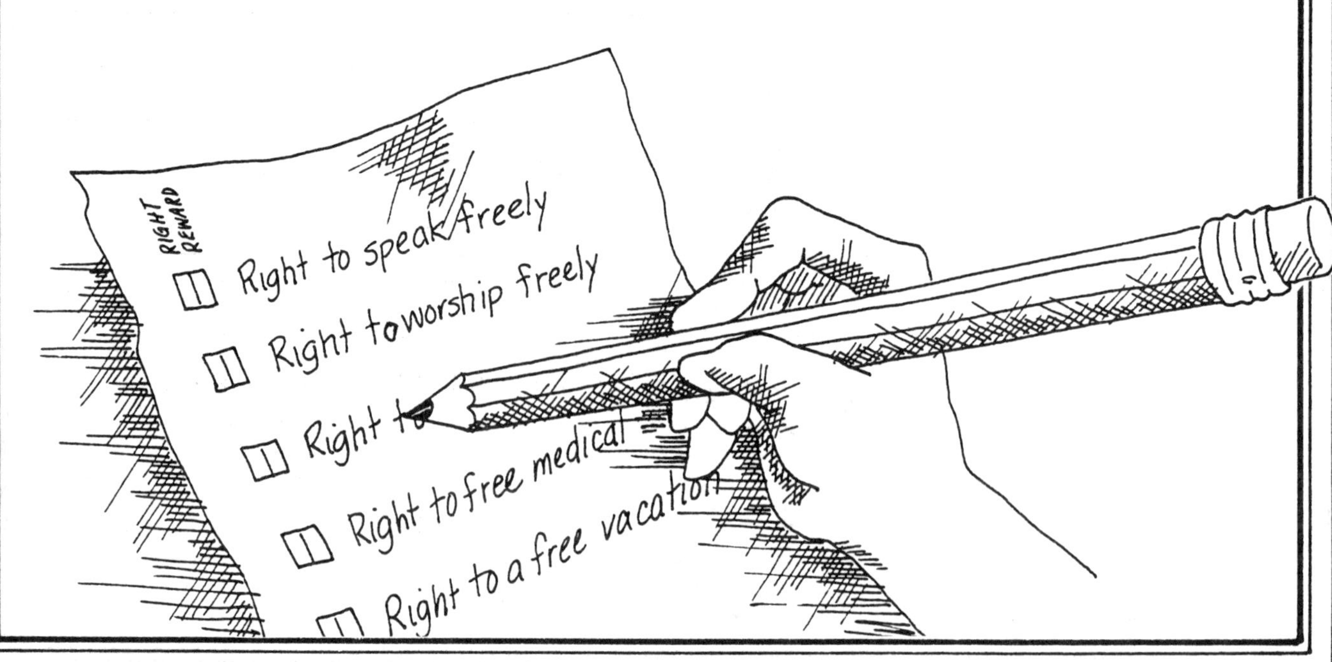

Name ____________

RIGHT VS. REWARD

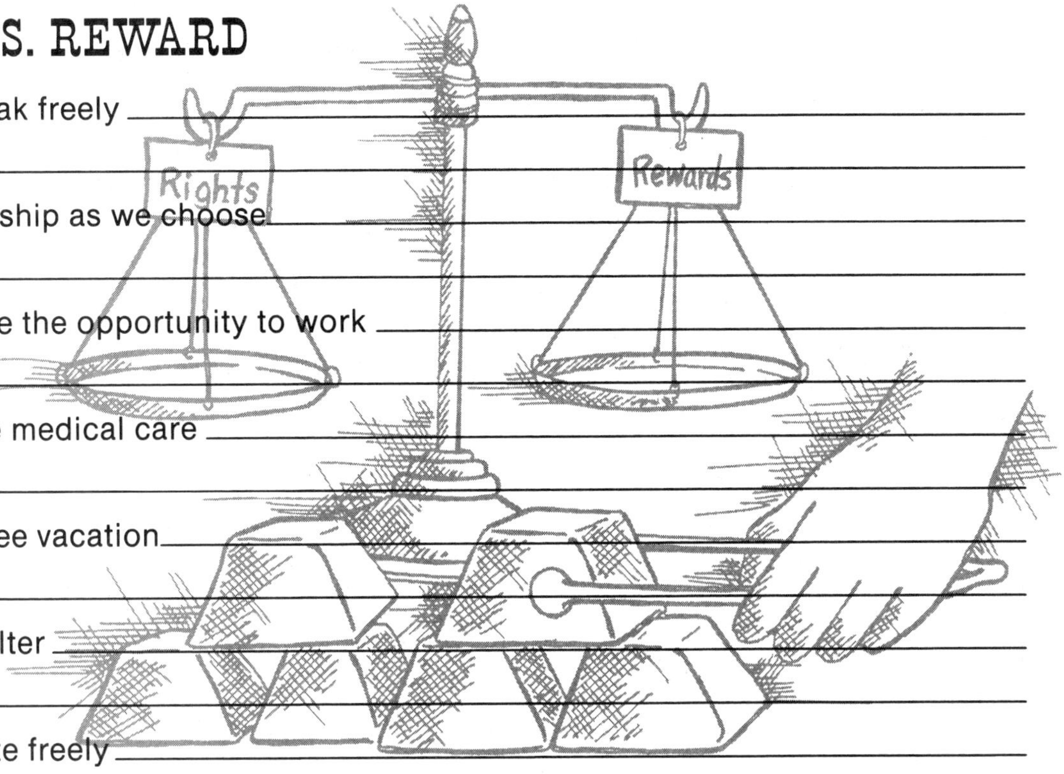

Right to speak freely ____________

Right to worship as we choose ____________

Right to have the opportunity to work ____________

Right to free medical care ____________

Right to a free vacation ____________

Right to shelter ____________

Right to write freely ____________

Right to openly criticize the actions of government ____________

Right to enjoy freedom from hunger ____________

Right to vote freely for candidate of choice ____________

Right to an eight-hour workday with extra pay for overtime ____________

Right to due process ____________

Right to circulate a petition to enlist support for a change in an existing law or a new one I propose ____________

Right to face in open court those who stand as my accusers ____________

Name ______________________

CAPITALISM, SOCIALISM AND COMMUNISM

Below are several statements that describe three of the world's most common political ideologies. Only when we compare the pluses and minuses of each system can we decide which we feel is best and most suitable for the people. Research the main economic and social conditions of each system, and then decide which statements best apply to each economic system. Place your choice in the blank space provided; then be prepared to comment on reasons for your choice.

1. ____________ The private enterprise system.
2. ____________ The community is the sole entrepreneur.
3. ____________ The state owns the instruments of production.
4. ____________ Small-scale private enterprise is permitted.
5. ____________ Various types of income are obtainable through hard work and ingenuity.
6. ____________ The sharing of wealth is according to need.
7. ____________ Profits through risk-taking and successful marketing are the rewards of this system.
8. ____________ The means of production are controlled and decisions are made by public authority.
9. ____________ Beating the competition is the name of the game.
10. ____________ There is private ownership, but it doesn't control the vitality of the economy.
11. ____________ In societies where it exists, revolution is characteristic in establishing its domination.
12. ____________ A "classless" society.
13. ____________ The production of private enterprise is regulated by the government but not to the point of destroying the competition the system thrives on.
14. ____________ A combination of public and private enterprise.
15. ____________ It favors evolutionary over revolutionary methods to establish itself.
16. ____________ Most individuals rely on compensation in the form of income for the rendering of personal service.
17. ____________ It comes closest to true democracy.

Name________________________________

CAPITALISM, SOCIALISM AND COMMUNISM

18. ___________ Because much of the land is publicly owned, there is very little income derived by individuals through rent.

19. ___________ Marx and Lenin are associated with its emergence as an economic system of government.

20. ___________ Consideration of supply and demand are important determinants of the wealth of the individuals.

Share and discuss your thoughts and choices with other members of your class.

From what you have read and learned from sharing with others, what is it that you will remember most about each of the systems? Jot down a single statement about each that best summarizes your own notions and means of identifying each of the economic systems.

Capitalism ________________________________

____

____

____

____

Socialism ________________________________

____

____

____

____

Communism ________________________________

____

____

____

____

____

____

____

____

CHOOSING OUR LEADERS

As a governmental system, democracy involves elections. The outcome of an election determines those who shall govern. However, the end result sometimes depends on the method used in the election process. That is why there is often controversy over the selection of a method. Direct elections are generally more the rule in democratic societies, but in the United States (certainly considered a democratic nation by today's standards) an indirect method to elect its President is used.

In a direct election, the people decide which candidate wins by simply expressing their choice from among those competing candidates. There are several methods that fit this description. Under the indirect plan, the people choose those who will officially select the officeholder. The Electoral College functions in this manner when it elects the President of the United States over a month after the people have expressed their personal choice.

It is also true that in today's democracies not everyone is automatically allowed to vote. Voting is considered a privilege and certain conditions must be met before a person becomes eligible to vote. The qualifying factors in a democracy must be liberal enough to allow most to qualify. Those qualifications usually involve age, citizenship and residence within the voting district as well as literacy, provided that adequate opportunity to overcome illiteracy is available to all persons. In the United States, simply being born here automatically satisfies the literacy requirement. It is assumed that everyone will have the opportunity to gain a proper education. Looking more closely at voter qualifications, let's examine the matter of citizenship. Why do we have such a requirement? Aliens owe their allegiance to their native homeland, and so it was reasoned. . . they just might exercise their voting privilege in such a manner that would promote their native country's interests first. Thus those people who do not automatically qualify as citizens through birth are required to take a literacy test and meet certain other requirements that will prove them worthy of becoming U.S. citizens.

Perhaps the first step in the electoral process is to determine who gets to vote. Not everyone who lives in the United States has the right to vote. Voting is considered a privilege, and certain criteria are used to determine those who are afforded this privilege.

Name ____________________

CHOOSING OUR LEADERS

1. Find out the qualifications for voting where you live and list the qualifications below.

____
____
____
____

2. Look at the list above. Which qualification(s) do you lack that disqualifies you from voting?

____
____
____
____

3. Once a potential voter qualifies by meeting the established criterion, he/she becomes a legitimate voter. What responsibilities do you attach to that right that go hand in hand with properly serving the democratic process?

____
____
____
____

ELECTING OUR PRESIDENT

Every four years on the second Tuesday in November, citizens of the United States vote for their President. The names of the candidates appear on the ballots (or voting machines) they use, but the people are actually voting for an entire slate of individuals who will later cast the votes that will decide who becomes President and Vice President. This group of voters is known as the Electoral College.

Our founding fathers were uncertain when faced with the decision of how our President should be chosen. There were some who favored leaving the decision up to the members of Congress. But that plan was set aside because it would have placed too much power in their hands. (Congress was already assigned the task of making our laws.) The men who wrote the Constitution were looking for a balance of power among the three branches of government.

Others felt that the President should be elected directly by the people. But that plan was also abandoned because there was a feeling that the common citizen would not be properly informed about those who were running for President. There was also concern among the smaller states that under this method, they would have little voice in deciding who would win.

Finally it was agreed that each state would be given the power to appoint a number of intermediate electors that was equal to the number of senators and representatives it had in Congress. These electors would then meet in their own states on a given day and vote for the man of their choice. The results would be sent to the U.S. Senate. The candidate winning the most votes would become President and the runner-up would become Vice President. If no candidate won a majority of the electoral votes, then the election would be decided by the House of Representatives. There each state would have a single vote. Voting would continue until a single candidate had a majority of votes. If there was a tie for the vice presidency (the runner-up), the U.S. Senate was given the responsibility of making the choice.

Name ______________________

ELECTING OUR PRESIDENT

Over the years changes have been made in the system. The popular vote of the people *does* count. Whereas the state legislators often chose the electors, and they voted as they saw fit, the voters of today are voting for a slate of electors that will truly represent the candidate of their choice. For example, if a state has 23 electors, there are 23 dedicated party members representing the Republican party and 23 equally dedicated party members to represent the Democratic party. There would also be 23 people designated to represent any strong third-party candidate. When the people go to the polls and express their choices, they are actually voting for the entire slate of electors that will represent their candidate. The candidate who receives the greatest majority of votes from the people is declared the winner of that state, and his entire slate of electors can vote for him in the election conducted by the Electoral College. The candidate who finishes in second place doesn't win anything! Even though he may come very close in the popular vote of the people, he doesn't get any of the electoral votes from that state. None of his electors are allowed to vote! It's purely a winner-take-all election, and the runner-up comes away with only the satisfaction of trying very hard.

1. Look at the map below. If you were running for President, in which states would you spend most of your campaign dollars and energy?

____

____

____

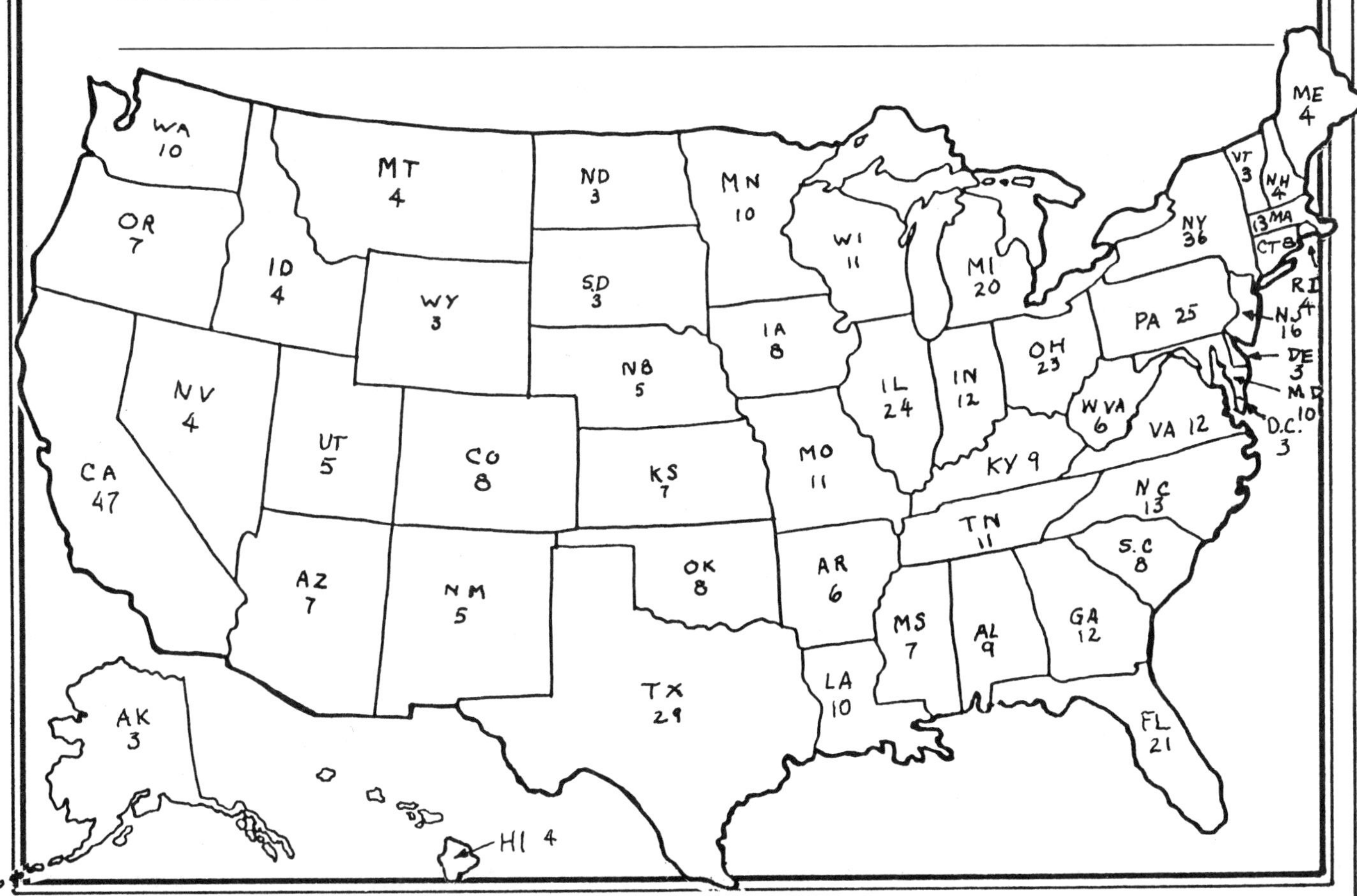

Name ______________________________

ELECTING OUR PRESIDENT

2. Why don't we hear much about major presidential campaigning in states like North Dakota, Nevada, Utah and Alaska?

____

____

____

____

____

____

3. Another change in the method of choosing our President today involves a candidate for President and a candidate for Vice President representing each major party. When Americans go to the polls, they are expressing their choice for a team. Can you think of any reasons for changing the system from the method used by the framers of the Constitution who determined that the runner-up in the election for President would become the Vice President?

____

____

____

____

____

____

____

____

____

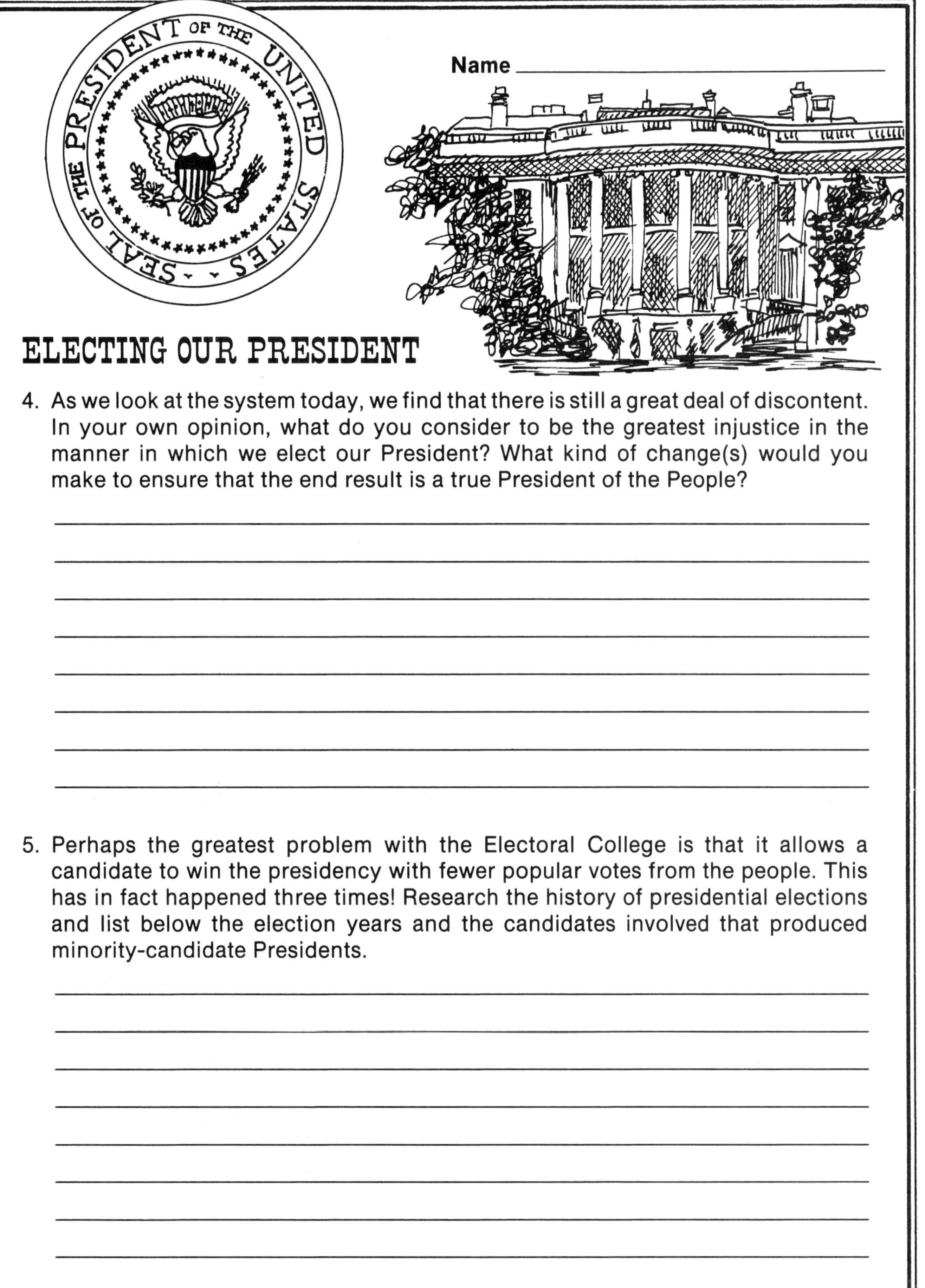

Name ____________________

ELECTING OUR PRESIDENT

4. As we look at the system today, we find that there is still a great deal of discontent. In your own opinion, what do you consider to be the greatest injustice in the manner in which we elect our President? What kind of change(s) would you make to ensure that the end result is a true President of the People?

____
____
____
____
____
____
____
____

5. Perhaps the greatest problem with the Electoral College is that it allows a candidate to win the presidency with fewer popular votes from the people. This has in fact happened three times! Research the history of presidential elections and list below the election years and the candidates involved that produced minority-candidate Presidents.

____
____
____
____
____
____
____
____

Name ______________________

THE ELECTORAL DISTRIBUTION

Place the two-letter abbreviation used by the U.S. Postal Service within the border of each state. Then find out the number of electoral votes that state had in the last presidential election and place that number beneath the state's abbreviation.

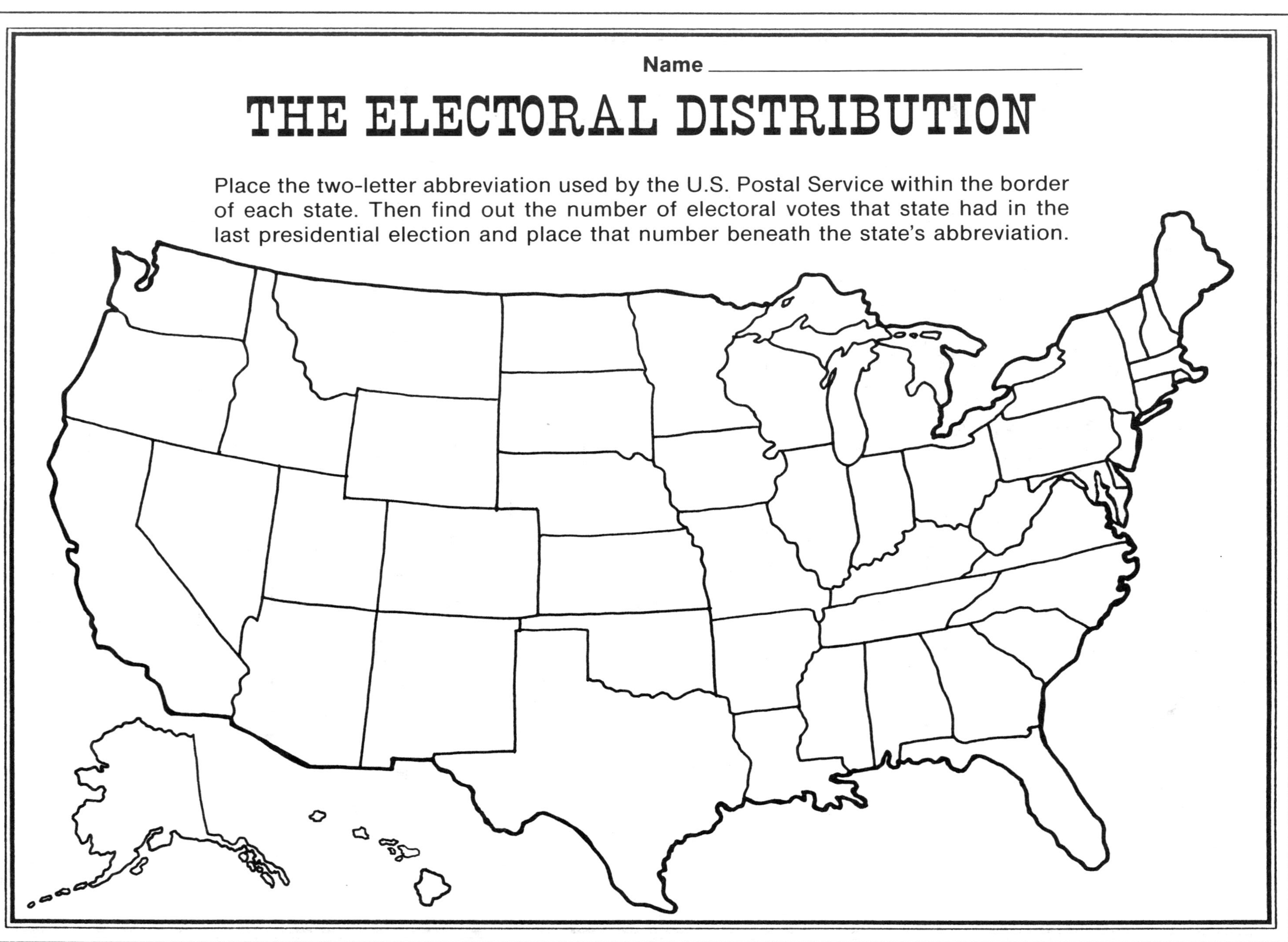

Name ______________________________

BOTH SIDES OF THE AISLE

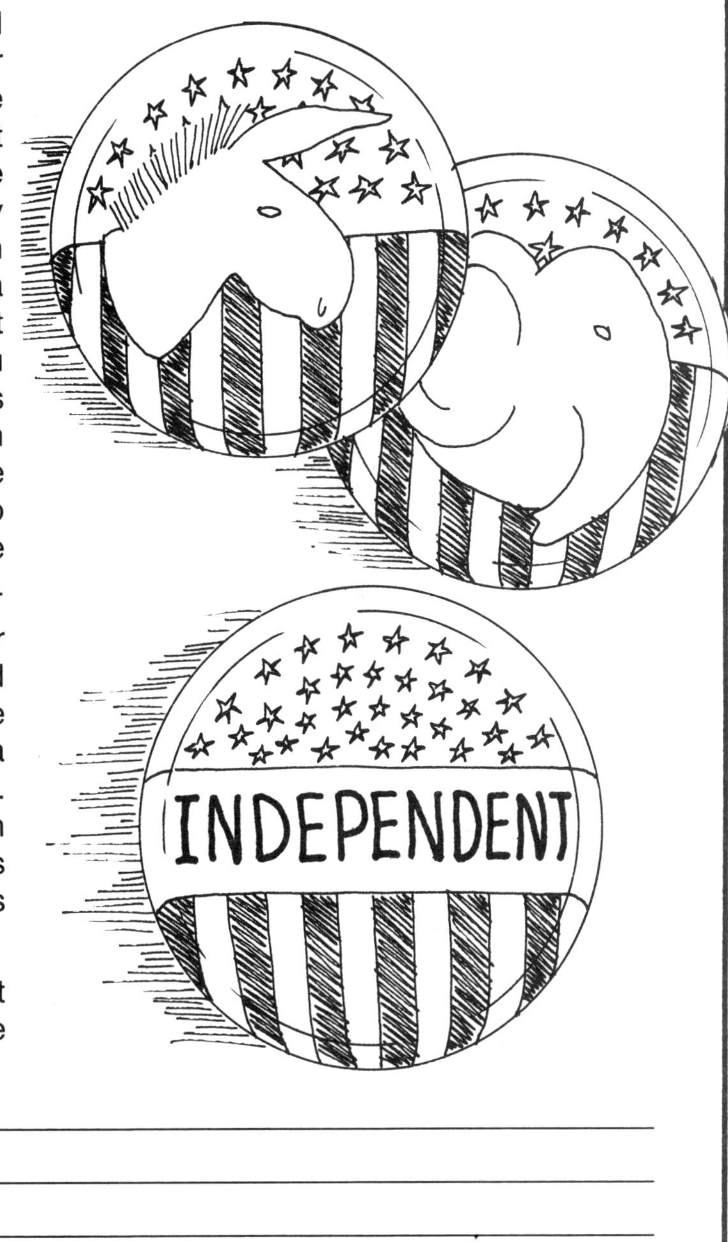

Let's assume that you have established yourself as a legitimate candidate for President. The fact that you won the race for governor as an independent says a lot for your popularity with the people. Yet no President in the history of this great country has ever been elected without the endorsement of a major political party. As you look at the impossible task before you, you decide that you must choose what's best for you (because of your own beliefs). . . and then you must figure out a way to portray those feelings to people in both parties who might be influenced by what they see and hear.

Since you aren't a member of either major party, you won't be subjected to the pressures that are put on the major-party candidates to push a certain way for issues dear to the party. You will in fact build your own platform based purely on your own beliefs about what this great country needs to become even greater.

List below the six most important issues upon which you wish to take a stand.

____

____

____

____

____

____

____

____

____

Name ______________________________

ELECTION DAY

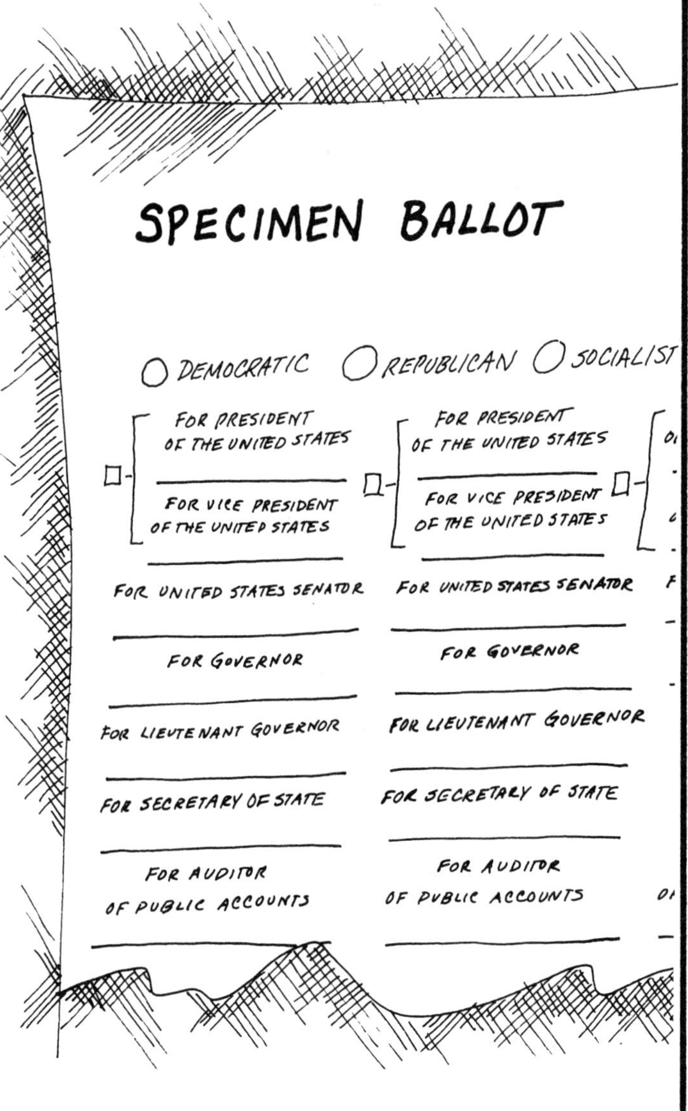

SPECIMEN BALLOT
DEMOCRATIC
REPUBLICAN
SOCIALIST
FOR PRESIDENT OF THE UNITED STATES
FOR VICE PRESIDENT OF THE UNITED STATES
FOR PRESIDENT OF THE UNITED STATES
FOR VICE PRESIDENT OF THE UNITED STATES
FOR UNITED STATES SENATOR
FOR UNITED STATES SENATOR
FOR GOVERNOR
FOR GOVERNOR
FOR LIEUTENANT GOVERNOR
FOR LIEUTENANT GOVERNOR
FOR SECRETARY OF STATE
FOR SECRETARY OF STATE
FOR AUDITOR OF PUBLIC ACCOUNTS
FOR AUDITOR OF PUBLIC ACCOUNTS

Every four years on the second Tuesday in November the people of the United States vote for President. The names of the candidates appear on the ballot, but the voters are really voting for an entire slate of individuals who will later cast the actual votes that determine who will become the President and Vice President. Although we believe very strongly in the democratic process of free elections, we the people do not directly elect our President. The election is officially done in the Electoral College.

To explain the background of this rather strange and often unpopular procedure, we must reflect back into history to America's founding fathers. Their feeling was that the state legislatures would be the most knowledgeable about the candidates and therefore should have the decision. This decision was rejected, however, because opponents felt it would place too much power in the hands of the legislative branch of our government. To keep the plan of checks and balances in perspective, they wanted the election to be outside the hands of the lawmakers.

1. It was suggested by some of the delegates that the people themselves should elect the President. It would certainly seem that this would be the obvious procedure for a young emerging nation founded on the principles of real democracy. But it didn't work out that way. Find out the reason the framers of the Constitution refused to allow the people to vote directly for their President.

____

____

____

Name ____________________

ELECTION DAY

2. The men who wrote the Constitution finally devised a plan called the Electoral College. Under this proposal, the people themselves did not participate directly in electing their President, but neither was it passed into the hands of the lawmakers. It was instead a compromise where intermediate electors would cast the real ballots. Each state was granted the power to choose its electors by whatever method it chose. The electors would then choose the President. All states did not have the same number of electors. Find out how it was decided the number of electors each state would be allowed and describe the method below.

3. Under the original plan of the Constitution, the electors would meet in their respective states on a given day and cast votes for two candidates. The results would be sent to the U.S. Senate to be counted. The candidate with the most votes became President and the candidate with the second greatest number of votes was elected Vice President. Unfortunately, this theory did not work very well in the real world. Find out what has changed from this method in which the Electoral College elected our President and Vice President.

4. While the founding fathers meant well, their reasoning was not very good on the matter of the election of the Vice President. Think about the implications of the method they chose and briefly describe the problems of the plan.

5. Compare the method of choosing the President under the original Constitution with the procedure used today for choosing electors.

6. What procedure is used in the event that no candidate wins a majority of the electoral votes?

THE ELECTORAL COLLEGE TODAY

As the young nation went through its first few elections, few people even voted for President. In several of the states the electors were chosen by the state legislators. And in those states where popular votes were conducted, the results had little to do with how the electors actually voted, as the popular vote did not dictate their choices.

Down through the years many changes have somewhat improved the electoral system from the process of those early years. Today the popular vote of the people does count. When a citizen casts a vote for a candidate, that person is actually voting for an entire slate of electors that are pledged to vote for that candidate. If Candidate A wins more of the popular votes than Candidate B, then all of Candidate A's electors from that state get to vote in the Electoral College and none of Candidate B's electors are allowed to vote. This is why the popular votes held in fifty states and in Washington, D.C., on election day are so important. These elections determine who the President will be because they are directing the slate of electors in each state (and in the nation's capital) that will vote in the Electoral College.

Name ______________________________

THE ELECTORAL COLLEGE TODAY

1. While this procedure is certainly more becoming to a nation calling itself a democracy than the way things were formerly done, the Electoral College continues to fall under the attack of critics who say it isn't fair. Analyze carefully the procedures used and describe your own feelings about why the Electoral College is still unfair.

____
____
____
____
____
____

2. Describe two hypothetical situations in which a "minority candidate" could win the presidency.

____
____
____
____
____
____
____
____
____

3. How would you change procedures used in the Electoral College today to make it more fair and democratic if the opportunity were suddenly delegated to you? Consider all the historical injustices that have occurred as a result of its present structure.

____
____
____
____
____
____

CONSERVATISM VS. LIBERALISM VS. REPUBLICANISM

To gain a better understanding of the policies and philosophies of the various political groups that function in our society today, we need to probe back into the ideologies of the nineteenth century. By doing this, we can see which groups and classes supported each of the different political positions and their reasons for doing so. In reality the relationships within social groups were sometimes fairly complicated. But if we can get some general base ideas in mind about each philosophy, it will no doubt be easier to understand the reasons the various groups and subgroups had for their political loyalties.

Name ______________________

CONSERVATISM VS. LIBERALISM VS. REPUBLICANISM

Below are several basic-position statements of nineteenth century *conservatives* and *liberals*. (Liberalism in the nineteenth century was different from its meaning today.) Consult a good history text and read about the background of the various groups listed below; then decide whether that group would have supported *conservatism* or *liberalism* or *republicanism* as a political philosophy. Place your choice (C) for conservatism, (L) for liberalism or (R) for republicanism in the blank space provided.

___ 1. The landed aristocracy
___ 2. They felt that farming was the most honorable of occupations.
___ 3. Those in the business and industrial world
___ 4. They felt that voting rights and the right to hold a public office should be limited to those who were educated and owned property.
___ 5. Popular among the lower middle class
___ 6. They felt that a solid future hinged upon science and invention.
___ 7. Favored by the young whose incomes were modest
___ 8. Believed that the hearts of all people were good and would be guided toward right decisions
___ 9. Felt that the wealthy had no reason to profit from politics and would thus serve all people well
___ 10. They believed that government should control business and industry.
___ 11. Their political ideal was more that of true democracy than either of the other two philosophies.
___ 12. The power should rest in the hands of an assembly elected directly by the people.
___ 13. They pushed for regulation of working conditions and established hours in factories.
___ 14. They were against government intervention except to deal with problems caused by strikers and labor organizations.
___ 15. They believed that history moves in cycles, that better times were followed by worse times, and the worse times were replaced by better times.
___ 16. Civil servants, small store owners and lower income workers favored this philosophy.
___ 17. They both feared and dreaded the results of the Industrial Revolution.
___ 18. People who were in the upper middle class social strata tended toward this philosophy.
___ 19. They believed certain people were "born to rule" and those people should be the leaders.
___ 20. Their politics rejected *laissez-faire* and called for widespread civil rights and freedoms for the people.

THE ROAD TO THE WHITE HOUSE

While Election Day is quite obviously the most important day to the candidates in their drive for the presidency, it actually is the culmination of many, many hours and days that began months—even years—before. For an incumbent, the job of getting his name before the public is simple. It's already there. But for someone who is known only locally, or even regionally, the task of making his name a "household word" requires a lot of hard work, a lot of support from workers and many dollars. Down through the history of the presidency we've seen a lot of different theories and approaches used by those attempting to get to "know the people." It is interesting to look at the methods they've used and then put them into proper historical perspective. Once these campaigns are surrounded with the issues of the day in their proper time frame, it's usually fairly simple to figure out why the winning candidates won.

Research any two of the following presidential elections listed below:

Election of 1828
Election of 1860
Election of 1912
Election of 1924
Election of 1932
Election of 1948
Election of 1964
Election of 1968
Election of 1976

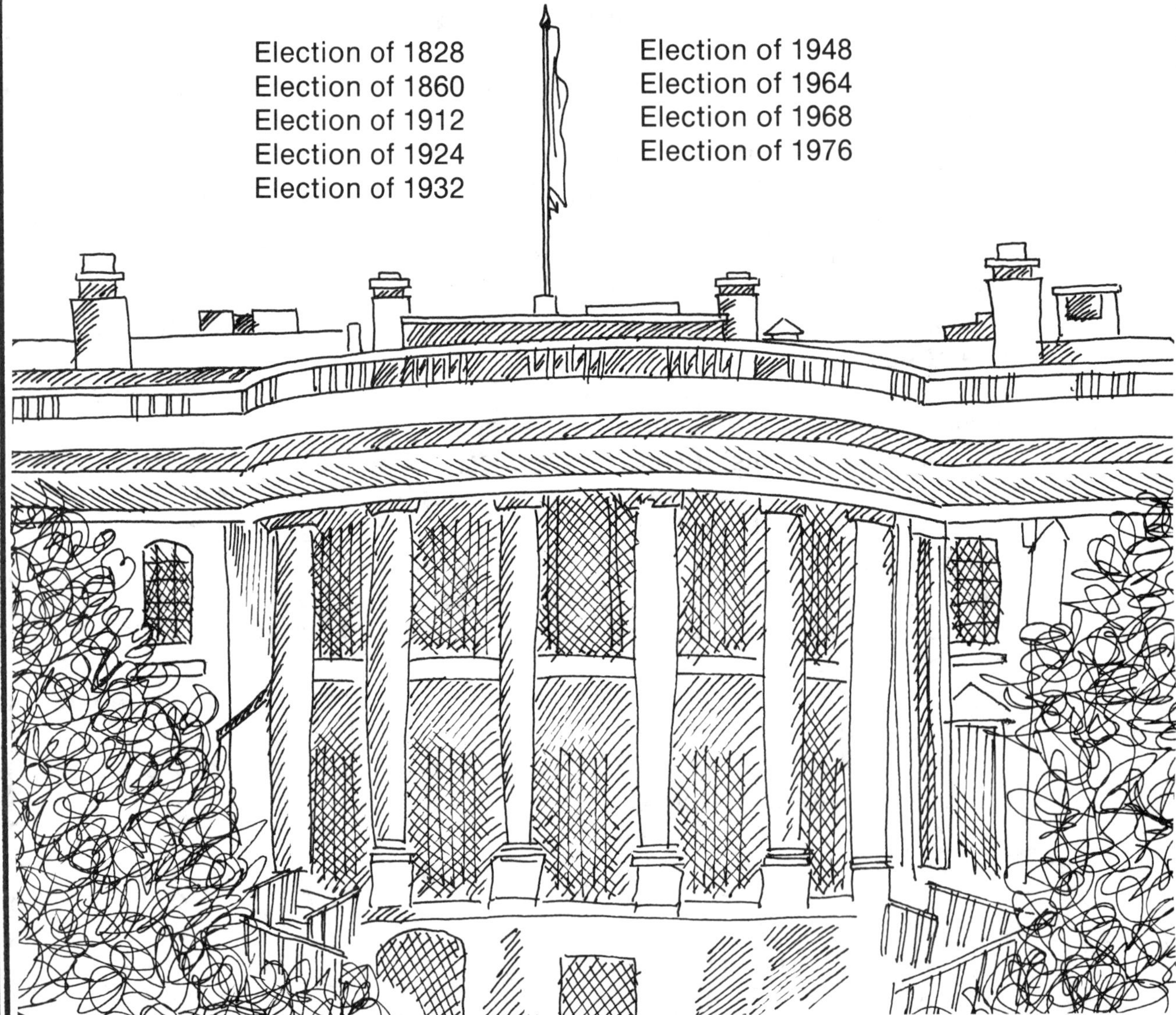

Name ____________________

THE ROAD TO THE WHITE HOUSE

As you read, you should be looking for answers to these questions.

What were the key issues of the election?

During what historical period did the election take place?

What parties did the major candidates represent?

Were there events of the day that occurred which played into the hands of either of the candidates?

What methods were used by the leading candidates in their efforts to win votes from the people?

Finally, compare and contrast the campaigns of the two winning candidates. Which method do you prefer?

If the two winning candidates were pitted against each other today in an election for President, who would win? Why?

Name ______________________

MY HAT IN THE RING

Even though you have not been endorsed by either party, you have an outside chance to become the first President in history to win "on his own." You are, after all, the governor of your state and you have been a part of the national political scene long enough to be very well-known. You have accumulated enough money from your own resources and that of your political supporters to launch a serious campaign for President of the United States. A brief news conference is scheduled tomorrow night to announce your candidacy. The major networks thought enough of your chances to ensure their being there. They have promised to give you five minutes of "prime time" coverage.

In the space below write the speech you will make before the nation to announce your candidacy. Remember, it's free! Take advantage of it.

Name ____________________

THERE'S NO FREE LUNCH. . .

Of course candidates want to say what the people want to hear! That helps them to win votes. But they must also be concerned with their own conscience and feelings when they make their speeches, because a candidate, once in office, must attempt to live up to his campaign promises. There will be constant pressure by groups who expect "their" candidate to carry out their wishes. It's very easy to sit back and think about all the social and economic issues that should and should not be. However, each comes with a price tag.

If, for example, you are pushing for more money in welfare relief for senior citizens, your words will win votes among senior citizens. But somebody will have to pay for that additional welfare, and that either means higher taxes (which will not be well received by other voters) or getting the money from another source. Nothing is without cost or sacrifice.

Think for a few moments about a platform that you yourself could use in all good conscience if you were running for President. Point out those issues which you have strong opinions about, and prepare a short speech (4-5 minutes) in which you briefly outline your position on the issues currently at stake in America (as you see them).

Name ___________________________

A MATTER OF GOOD TASTE. . .

As candidates for the presidency travel around the country meeting the people, they give speeches that emphasize their own political stance on many issues. The campaign flavor must reflect party philosophy, but it must also be attuned to the local and timely needs of the people who live in various parts of the United States. Candidates *must* be sensitive to the needs of the people at the local level.

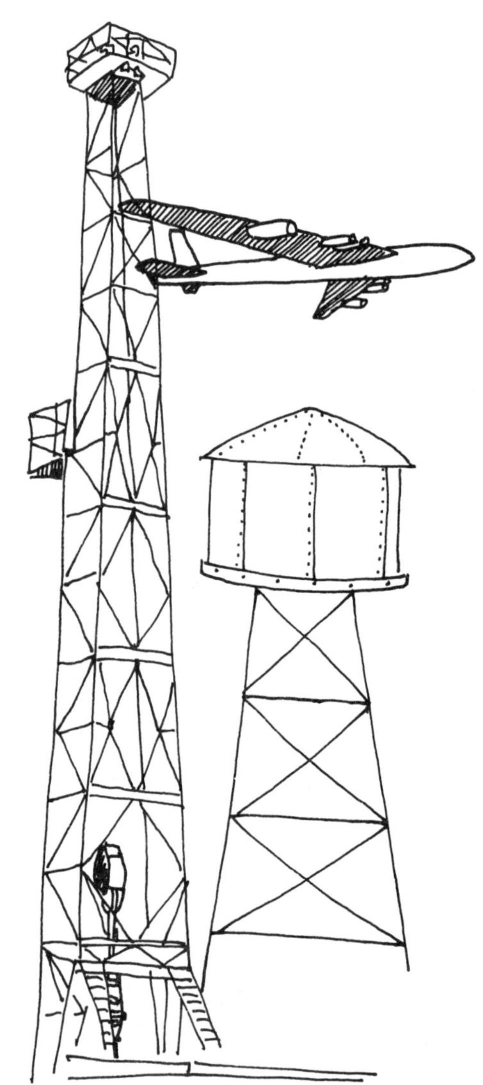

For example, if a candidate were campaigning in the Midwest, it would not be in his best interest to talk against subsidizing the farmer for not planting a portion of his land. Those running for President attempt to put themselves into a most favorable light among the people whenever and wherever they go. If you were running for President, what would you say to the people on each of the following issues:

The foreign trade issue in Detroit

____

____

____

____

Offshore drilling in Louisiana

____

____

____

____

Name ______________________

A MATTER OF GOOD TASTE. . .

Fishing rights in Maine and Massachusetts

Disposition of chemical wastes in Cleveland

Clean water rights in Minnesota

Dealing with illegal aliens in Texas

Consideration of a luxury tax on hotel/motel rooms in Hilton Head, South Carolina

Clean air standards in Los Angeles

GA1083

Name ______________________

SENSITIVE ISSUES

When candidates for President campaign in different parts of the country, they must constantly be aware of the problems and concerns that are most important to the people living in those areas. On the map below, draw a line from each state that has been shaded to the issue you feel would be of greatest concern to the people of that state.

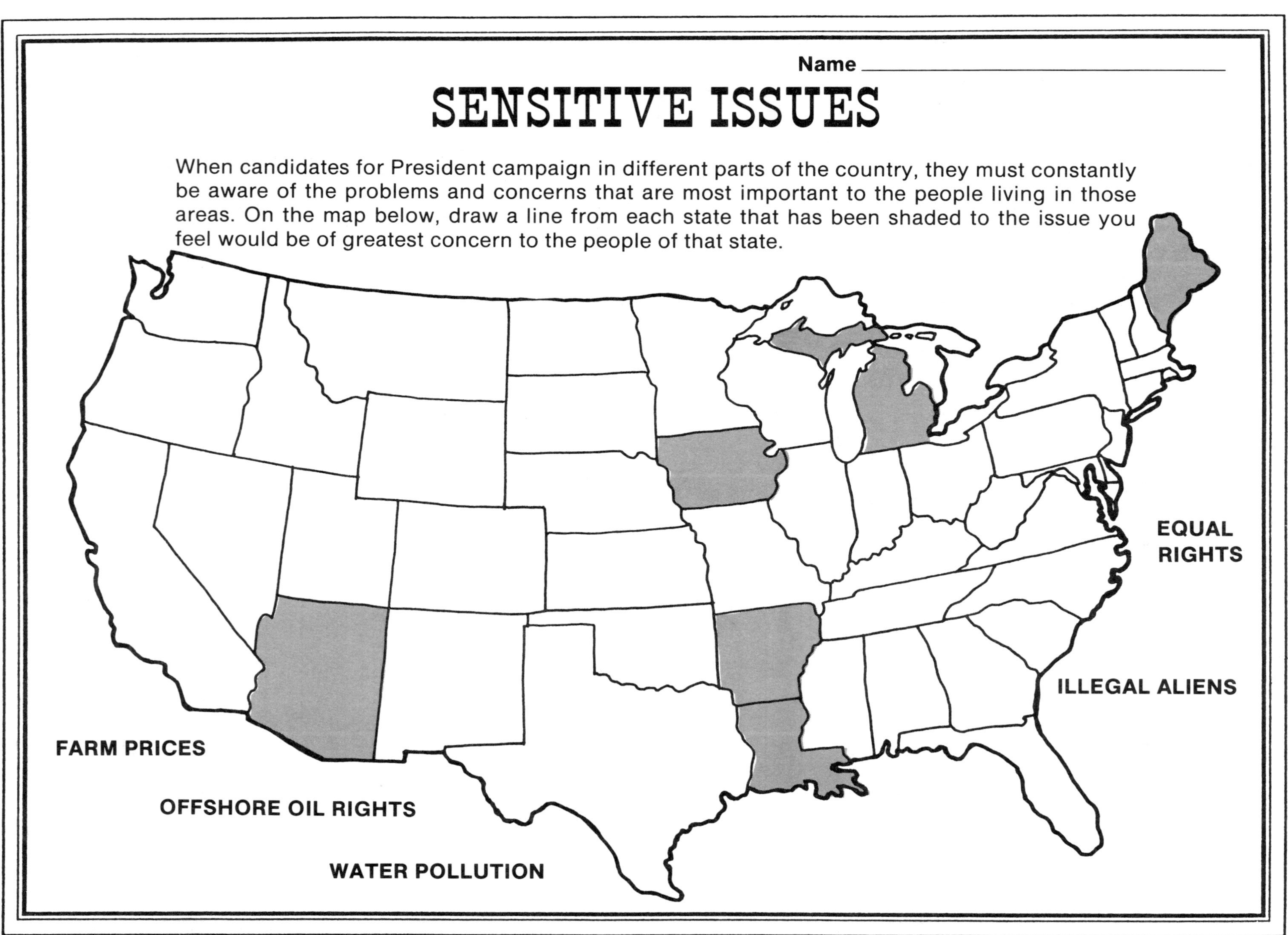

Name ______________________________

ISSUES OF CONCERN

Voting for our choices for public office is one of the many benefits of living in a democracy. Deciding who we are going to vote for can sometimes be a difficult decision. Some of us stick pretty much to the candidates that represent our political party loyalty. Others are more interested in the personalities of the candidates themselves. There are indeed candidates we sometimes vote for because they are charming or charismatic. . . or because they simply "look good." But there really *are* voters who base their decisions on the way candidates feel about issues that occupy the voters' priorities.

Candidates want to say what the people want to hear. That helps them to win votes. But those same voters will hold their candidates to live up to their promises once they're in office. Below are some of the more important issues that continually cause problems for our nation as a whole. Rank order them according to your own priorities. Then explain the importance of your first choice.

_____The Middle East

_____Foreign Trade

_____A Balanced Budget

_____A Cleaner Environment

_____Arms Control

_____National Health

_____Farm Economy

_____Pro-Life

I feel the most important concern to the people of this country today is__________

because____

____

____

____

____

____

____

____

____

Name ______________________

IF I WERE PRESIDENT. . .

When candidates for President hit the campaign trail, they present themselves before the people in a way that will leave a positive impression. They tell people what they plan on doing to make the nation healthier and more prosperous once they are elected President. Imagine yourself a candidate for President. Write your own platform of the promises you would make to the people to win their votes. Remember that you cannot just make idle promises! Once elected, the people will hold you accountable for attempting to fulfill those promises.

Name ______________________________

ELECTION TRIVIA

Below are clues that will tell you the names to be looking for in the word search at the bottom of the page. Hidden are the names of ten past Presidents. You may find their names by moving your pencil forward, backward, or diagonally. Circle each name that answers one of the clues.

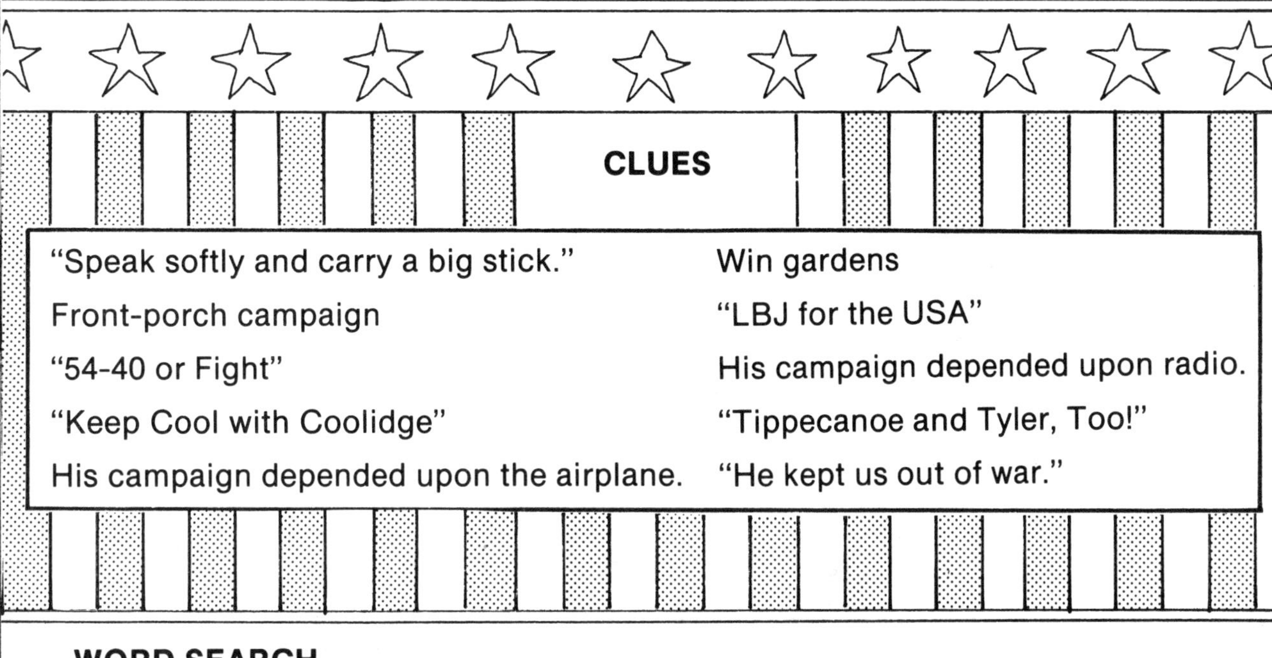

CLUES
"Speak softly and carry a big stick."
Front-porch campaign
"54-40 or Fight"
"Keep Cool with Coolidge"
His campaign depended upon the airplane.
Win gardens
"LBJ for the USA"
His campaign depended upon radio.
"Tippecanoe and Tyler, Too!"
"He kept us out of war."

WORD SEARCH

I J C M R L B S R K M N V
M O A O R Y O H O P O M T
R H R P O U M A N S T C B
T N T P O L K F L L R K V
S S E S S O I I N T P I A
F O R D E W W D D O Q N O
O N O O V F V U G G O L C
V A C R E V O O H E G E F
O M R S L L E Y R E L Y T
E I R F T M M L T U L M P

Name ____________________

POLL WATCHING

Political polls are used by the news media to gauge the popularity of candidates among the people for approaching elections. Their importance seems to surface most during presidential election years. Political parties use opinion polls to learn about their candidates' strengths and weaknesses, and they help parties to plan campaign strategies. The method most often used is to test a small sampling of potential voters; then from that, they forecast a similar trend among all the voters. Polls can be of value, but the validity of the sample is most important if the poll is to be a legitimate barometer of the voting public.

Look at the information on the graphic presentation of a poll below.

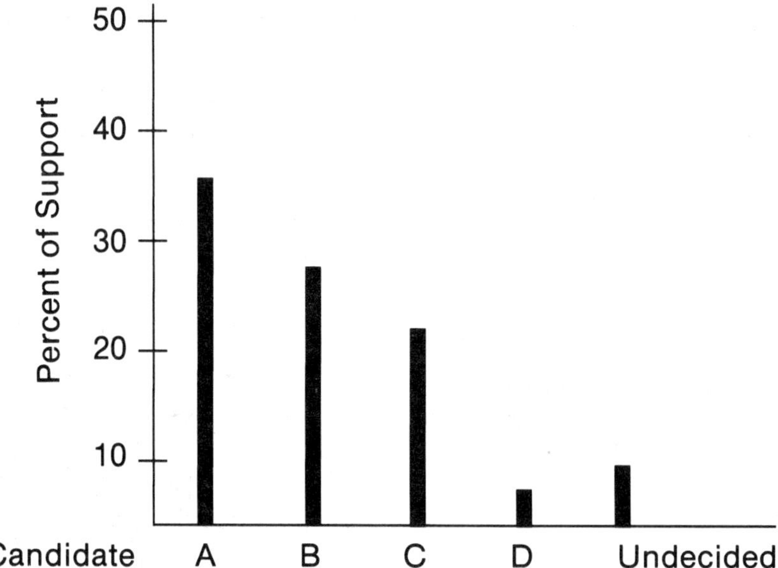

1. According to the information contained in this poll, which candidate is leading? ____________________
2. How much support (percentage of voters) is there for Candidate C? ____________________
3. What percentage of the people are undecided? ____________________
4. What use will supporters of Candidate A probably make of the survey? ____________________
5. How do you think Candidate B will use this information? ____________________
6. What advice do you have for Candidate C? ____________________
7. What advice do you have for Candidate D? ____________________

ELECTIONS OF THE PAST

Look carefully at the information on past presidential election results presented below and on the following pages. Then answer the questions that follow, based on that information.

Year	# of States	Candidates	Parties	Electoral Vote	% of Popular Vote
1789	11	GEORGE WASHINGTON	no party affiliations	69	—
			John Adams	34	
			Other Candidates	35	
1792	15	GEORGE WASHINGTON	Federalist	132	—
		John Adams	Federalist	77	
		George Clinton	Democratic-Republican	50	
		Other Candidates		5	
1796	16	JOHN ADAMS	Federalist	71	—
		Thomas Jefferson	Democratic-Republican	68	
		Thomas Pinckney	Federalist	59	
		Aaron Burr	Anti-Federalist	30	
		Other Candidates		48	
1800	16	THOMAS JEFFERSON	Democratic-Republican	73	—
		Aaron Burr	Democratic-Republican	73	
		John Adams	Federalist	65	
		Charles C. Pinckney	Federalist	64	
		John Jay	Federalist	1	
1804	17	THOMAS JEFFERSON	Democratic-Republican	162	—
		Charles C. Pinckney	Federalist	14	
1808	17	JAMES MADISON	Democratic-Republican	122	—
		Charles C. Pinckney	Federalist	47	
		George Clinton	Independent Republican	6	
1812	18	JAMES MADISON	Democratic-Republican	128	—
		DeWitt Clinton	Fusion	89	
1816	19	JAMES MONROE	Republican	183	—
		Rufus King	Federalist	34	
1820	24	JAMES MONROE	Republican	231	—
		John Quincy Adams	Independent Republican	1	
1824	24	JOHN QUINCY ADAMS	no party designation	84	30.5
		Andrew Jackson	no party designation	99	43.1
		William H. Crawford	no party designation	41	13.1
		Henry Clay	no party designation	37	13.2
1828	24	ANDREW JACKSON	Democratic	178	56.0
		John Quincy Adams	National Republican	83	44.0
1832	24	ANDREW JACKSON	Democratic	219	55.0
		Henry Clay	National Republican	49	42.4
		William Wirt	Anti-Masonic	7	8.0
		John Floyd	Nullifiers	11	—
1836	26	MARTIN VAN BUREN	Democratic	170	50.9
		William H. Harrison	Whig	73	36.6
		Hugh L. White	Whig	26	9.7
		Daniel Webster	Whig	14	2.8
		Willie P. Mangum	Anti-Jackson	11	—
1840	26	WILLIAM H. HARRISON	Whig	234	53.1
		Martin Van Buren	Democratic	60	46.9
1844	26	JAMES POLK	Democratic	170	49.6
		Henry Clay	Whig	105	48.1
		James G. Birney	Liberty	—	2.3

ELECTIONS OF THE PAST

Year	# of States	Candidates	Parties	Electoral Vote	% of Popular Vote
1848	30	ZACHARY TAYLOR	Whig	163	47.4
		Lewis Cass	Democratic	127	42.5
		Martin Van Buren	Free Soil	—	10.1
1852	31	FRANKLIN PIERCE	Democratic	254	50.9
		Winfield Scott	Whig	42	44.1
		John P. Hale	Free Soil	—	5.0
1856	31	JAMES BUCHANAN	Democratic	174	45.3
		John C. Fremont	Republican	114	33.1
		Millard Fillmore	American	8	21.6
1860	33	ABRAHAM LINCOLN	Republican	180	39.8
		Stephen A. Douglas	Democratic	12	29.5
		John C. Breckenridge	Democratic	72	18.1
		John Bell	Constitutional Union	39	12.6
1864	36	ABRAHAM LINCOLN	Republican	212	55.0
		George B. McClellan	Democratic	21	45.0
1868	37	ULYSSES S. GRANT	Republican	214	52.7
		Horatio Seymour	Democratic	80	47.3
1872	37	ULYSSES S. GRANT	Republican	286	55.6
		Horace Greeley	Democratic	—	43.9
		Other Candidates		63	—
1876	38	RUTHERFORD B. HAYES	Republican	185	48.0
		Samuel J. Tilden	Democratic	184	51.0
1880	38	JAMES A. GARFIELD	Republican	214	48.5
		Winfield S. Hancock	Democratic	155	48.1
		James B. Weaver	Greenback-Labor	—	3.4
1884	38	GROVER CLEVELAND	Democratic	219	48.5
		James G. Blaine	Republican	182	48.2
		Benjamin F. Butler	Greenback-Labor	—	1.8
		John P. St. John	Prohibition	—	1.5
1888	38	BENJAMIN HARRISON	Republican	233	47.9
		Grover Cleveland	Democratic	168	48.6
		Clinton B. Fisk	Prohibition	—	2.2
		Anson J. Streeter	Union Labor	—	1.3
1892	44	GROVER CLEVELAND	Democratic	277	46.1
		Benjamin Harrison	Republican	145	43.0
		James B. Weaver	People's	22	8.5
		John Bidwell	Prohibition	—	2.2
1896	45	WILLIAM McKINLEY	Republican	271	51.1
		William J. Bryan	Democratic	176	47.7
1900	45	WILLIAM MCKINLEY	Republican	292	51.7
		William J. Bryan	Democratic	155	45.5
		John C. Wooley	Prohibition	—	1.5
1904	45	THEODORE ROOSEVELT	Republican	336	57.4
		Alton B. Parker	Democratic	140	37.6
		Eugene V. Debs	Socialist	—	3.0
		Silas C. Swallow	Prohibition	—	1.9
1908	46	WILLIAM H. TAFT	Republican	321	51.6
		William J. Bryan	Democratic	162	43.1
		Eugene V. Debs	Socialist	—	2.8
		Eugene W. Chafin	Prohibition	—	1.7
1912	48	WOODROW WILSON	Democratic	435	41.9
		Theodore Roosevelt	Progressive	88	27.4
		William H. Taft	Republican	8	23.2
		Eugene V. Debs	Socialist	—	6.0
		Eugene W. Chafin	Prohibition	—	1.4

ELECTIONS OF THE PAST

Year	# of States	Candidates	Parties	Electoral Vote	% of Popular Vote
1916	48	WOODROW WILSON	Democratic	277	49.4
		Charles E. Hughes	Republican	254	46.2
		A. L. Benson	Socialist	—	3.2
		J. Frank Hanly	Prohibition	—	1.2
1920	48	WARREN G. HARDING	Republican	404	60.4
		James N. Cox	Democratic	127	34.1
		Eugene V. Debs	Socialist	—	3.4
		P.P. Christensen	Farmer-Labor	—	1.0
1924	48	CALVIN COOLIDGE	Republican	382	54.0
		John W. Davis	Democratic	136	28.8
		Robert LaFollette	Progressive	13	16.6
1928	48	HERBERT C. HOOVER	Republican	444	58.1
		Alfred E. Smith	Democratic	87	40.8
1932	48	FRANKLIN D. ROOSEVELT	Democratic	472	57.4
		Herbert C. Hoover	Republican	59	39.7
		Norman Thomas	Socialist	—	2.2
1936	48	FRANKLIN D. ROOSEVELT	Democratic	523	60.8
		Alfred M. Landon	Republican	8	36.5
		William Lemke	Union	—	1.9
1940	48	FRANKLIN D. ROOSEVELT	Democratic	449	54.7
		Wendell L. Willkie	Republican	82	44.8
1944	48	FRANKLIN D. ROOSEVELT	Democratic	432	53.4
		Thomas E. Dewey	Republican	99	45.9
1948	48	HARRY S. TRUMAN	Democratic	303	49.6
		Thomas E. Dewey	Republican	189	45.1
		J. Strom Thurmond	States' Rights	39	2.4
		Henry A. Wallace	Progressive	—	2.4
1952	48	DWIGHT D. EISENHOWER	Republican	442	55.1
		Adlai E. Stevenson	Democratic	89	44.4
1956	48	DWIGHT D. EISENHOWER	Republican	457	57.4
		Adlai E. Stevenson	Democratic	73	42.0
1960	50	JOHN F. KENNEDY	Democratic	303	49.7
		Richard M. Nixon	Republican	219	49.5
1964	50	LYNDON B. JOHNSON	Democratic	486	61.1
		Barry M. Goldwater	Republican	52	38.5
1968	50	RICHARD M. NIXON	Republican	301	43.4
		Hubert H. Humphrey	Democratic	191	42.7
		George C. Wallace	American Independent	46	13.5
1972	50	RICHARD M. NIXON	Republican	520	60.7
		George S. McGovern	Democratic	17	37.5
		John G. Schmitz	American	—	1.4
1976	50	JIMMY CARTER	Democratic	297	50.1
		Gerald R. Ford	Republican	240	48.0
1980	50	RONALD REAGAN	Republican	489	50.7
		Jimmy Carter	Democratic	49	41.0
		John B. Anderson	National Unity	—	6.6
		Ed Clark	Libertarian	—	1.1
1984	50	RONALD REAGAN	Republican	525	58.8
		Walter Mondale	Democratic	13	40.6
1988	50	GEORGE BUSH	Republican	426	53.8
		Michael Dukakis	Democratic	112	46.1

Name ____________________

ELECTIONS OF THE PAST

On a separate sheet of paper, answer the following questions:

1. When was the first popular vote of people conducted in a presidential election?
2. Who was the last Federalist elected President?
3. When was there a tie among the electors voting for President?
4. Which President won the greatest percentage of popular votes among the people?
5. Which President was the first to win the presidency while losing the popular vote of the people?
6. Which election was the first in which the size of the United States was as it is today?
7. Which President was the first to be elected by the House of Representatives?
8. How many states were there when Abraham Lincoln was first elected President?
9. Which President was elected the greatest number of times?
10. How many different men have been elected President of the United States?
11. Which President was elected twice but not to two consecutive terms?
12. Which candidate was the first from the Democratic-Republican party elected President?
13. After George Washington, who was the next (and only one since) candidate elected President without a party designation?
14. How many times in the history of the electoral system have candidates won the presidency while losing the popular vote of the people?
15. In which election was the popular vote of the people the closest?
16. Which President won the greatest number of electoral votes in the Electoral College?
17. Which President won the greatest victory in the Electoral College over his closest rival?
18. What is the fewest number of electoral votes won by a man who became President?
19. Who was the last President elected before the addition of Alaska and Hawaii as states?
20. Who was the first and only President associated with the Whig party?
21. In the 20th century which runner-up presidential candidate has won the fewest electoral votes?
22. Which of the Free Soil candidates ran the best race?
23. How many Presidents have been elected to at least two terms?
24. How many electoral votes were cast in the election of 1888?
25. How much better a race did Michael Dukakis run than Walter Mondale? (Use percentage of electoral votes won as your point of reference.)

Name ____________________

FAILURE OF THE ARTICLES OF CONFEDERATION

The American Revolution united the colonies for the sole purpose of winning their freedom from England. The result of the struggle away from the centralizing authority under which they had lived was the Articles of Confederation. But this framework for government simply did not work. There are a number of reasons for their failure, but perhaps the greatest cause of their failure was the fact that there was nothing very democratic about them in the first place. The very reason for which they had fought so hard (gaining their freedom) had resulted in a system that would not work because it was in reality against the principles of democracy.

Consult any good history text that contains the Articles of Confederation. Look closely at the design of the document. What general conclusions can you draw that support the thesis that the Articles of Confederation failed because they lacked the elements of a true democracy? Write your answer on another sheet of paper.

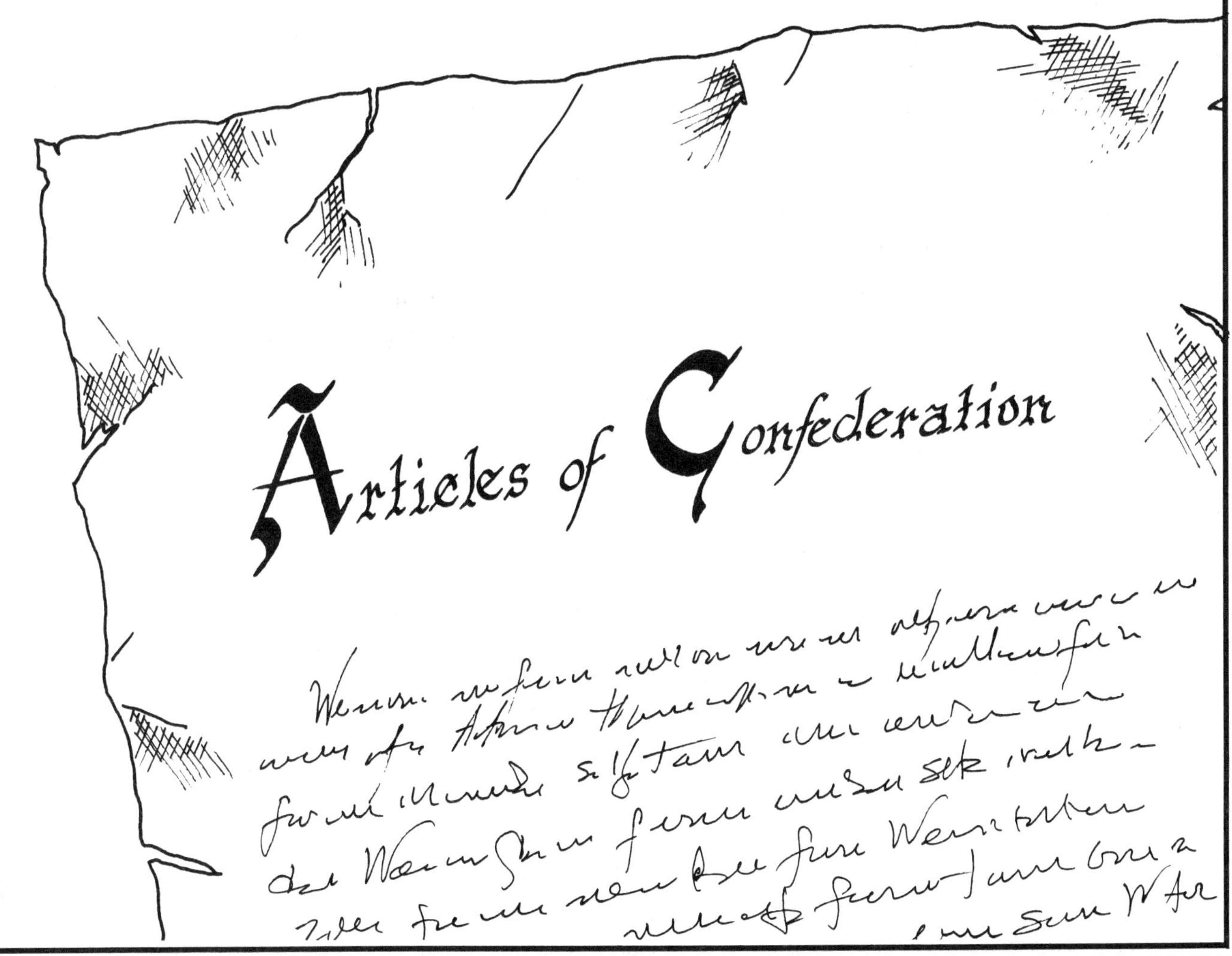

THE RIGHT OF DISSENT

In the spring of 1968, Paul Robert Cohen was arrested in the Los Angeles County courthouse for disorderly conduct. The cause for his arrest was the jacket he was wearing which had a vulgar message regarding the draft written on it. Authorities felt that wearing the jacket in a public place was offensive conduct. Cohen wore it because he wanted to let the public know how much he opposed the war in Vietnam. He claimed he was expressing his right of free speech guaranteed by the Constitution. Paul Cohen was convicted and sentenced to thirty days in jail. However, Cohen did not accept the decision and appealed his case through a series of courts until his arguments eventually reached the Supreme Court—the highest court in the United States.

The most important court has over five thousand cases submitted to it each year, but only actually hears about two hundred cases annually. Those cases which the court does select usually deal with fundamental issues of the law. The court chose to hear the case of Paul Cohen because it said that it dealt with protecting a person's expression of words—even though not spoken and offensive to some.

Freedom of speech does not give individuals the right to say or write anything they desire. There are limitations. If the words are likely to provoke a violent reaction, then such actions are not allowed. In the case of Paul Cohen, the court did not feel that the four-letter word on his jacket provoked anyone in particular. But it was offensive to some. However, the court felt that to decide to remove the word from the public vocabulary would be intrusion on freedom of expression. . . and could lead to all protests being disallowed simply because the majority didn't accept. If the government could censor particular words, then soon it might begin to suppress ideas. . . and before long it might come to use this power to censor or ban unpopular views.

Therefore, the Supreme Court reversed Paul Cohen's conviction and declared that he was only expressing his right of free speech—a right guaranteed to all American citizens.

Personal Liberty: Physical freedom to come and go as one pleases.

Religious Liberty: Freedom of worship and of private religious judgement.

Political Liberty: Right to vote.

Freedom of Speech: Freedom to voice opinions without interference, subject only to specific laws against. . .

Name ____________________

THE RIGHT OF DISSENT

1. One of the comments made in the opinion handed down by the Supreme Court was that ". . .it is nevertheless true that one man's vulgarity is another's lyric." What did Justice Harlon mean when he used these words?

____
____
____
____
____
____
____
____

2. The fact that Paul Cohen had chosen to express his loathing for the draft by using a vulgar four-letter word was not really the issue in this case. It would seem then that there are no restrictions in a person's right to free speech. This, however, is not true. Find out the critical issue in determining when a statement or expression is not allowed and when it becomes necessary to place restrictions on one's constitutional freedom of speech.

____
____
____
____
____
____
____
____

Name ____________________

THE RIGHT OF DISSENT

Divide the class into groups of three to five students each. The members of each group share with each other a situation which each student has "created" showing freedom of speech at stake. Each situation should be one in which the student who creates it feels there is a question of whether or not it should be allowed. Students in each group exchange their views on each situation—then they vote on whether or not it should be allowed. In each case the rule is that "the majority rules." Groups discuss the merits of each case. . . and their reasons for voting the way they voted.

____

____

____

____

. . . After discussion. . . A WRITTEN OPINION

Explain how the experience you had with your group parallels the operation of the Supreme Court. How does it arrive at its decisions? Is this the best way? How are the interactions among members of your group and the interactions among Supreme Court Justices examples of a democracy at work?

____

____

____

____

____

____

____

____

____

NEW YORK TIMES
New York City, New York
$1.50
Supreme Court Opinion
". . . It is nevertheless true that one man's vulgarity is another's lyric."

Name ____________________

TRIAL BY JURY

One of the most cherished words in a democracy is *fairness*. Decisions are made according to what is best for the group, because the group members are actually involved in making the decisions. Certainly those decisions won't please everyone, but they are ultimately made in such a manner that they will please *most* of the people. When it comes to deciding how to handle those people who break the laws of society and commit crimes that infringe upon the rights of others, such decisions are best left to a group of ordinary citizens.

That group of citizens is called a jury. A jury is made up of twelve people, and its members come from a random selection of all registered voters. The Constitution promises the right to be tried by a jury to all its citizens. The jury listens to both sides of the case. These twelve people then meet secretly to determine whether they feel the accused is guilty or not guilty. In most cases, all twelve people must agree. If they can't come to an agreement after many hours of trying, a *hung* jury is declared, and the case must be retried with a different jury.

The above right (to be tried by an impartial judgment or ordinary citizens) is all a part of living in a democracy. It is guaranteed to all of us in writing in the Sixth Amendment to the U.S. Constitution. That amendment includes other rights we have in court. Find the Sixth Amendment. Read carefully all that it says and list below the other rights that are found in the Sixth Amendment that are consistent with living in a democracy.

____

____

____

____

Name ____________________

CENSORSHIP: WHERE DO WE DRAW THE LINE?

Sometimes young people arrested for serious crimes, including murder, say they got the idea from watching television. This may sound like a cop-out on the part of the criminals, but psychologists have documented evidence that it *is* a fact that many heinous criminal acts have been committed as a result of violence viewed on TV. As a result, pressure groups have been formed all over the United States to try to cut down the amount of crime and violence available for viewing by our nation's youth. However, should we as a nation decide to prohibit such programming, we must look at the implications of possible violation of our personal rights.

The first amendment to the U.S. Constitution, which is the very cornerstone of this great democracy, clearly spells out our freedom of speech and expression. To impose censorship on our televiewing would be in direct conflict with that right in the eyes of many Americans.

On the other hand, our courts ruled that there are indeed restrictions placed upon our freedom of expression on many occasions and under certain circumstances. What is your opinion? Should there be a censoring agency that screens and edits programming to be aired on public television? If so, what, if any, are its limitations? What should be the last word in censorship? Does such action violate the principles of democracy even though it might prevent crime? Explain your own thoughts.

____

____

____

____

____

____

____

____

Name ____________________

CENSORSHIP: WHERE DO WE DRAW THE LINE?

While we may agree that censorship *does* involve, at least to a degree, a violation of principles etched into a true democracy, our freedom is sometimes very precious to us all. Yet we also recognize that there are certain unstable people in this country who watch television and are influenced into criminal acts. How would you feel if you, yourself, or a member of your family or a friend were to become the victim of a crime as the result of a program seen on television? Explain your answer from your own personal views and how you would feel.

____

____

____

____

____

____

____

____

____

____

Ask twelve people who are not in your class about their opinions. Ask them to respond to their choice of three questions:

1. Is censoring TV programming a violation of your constitutional rights?
2. Is outlawing graphic violence on TV okay if justified on the grounds that it prevents crime?
3. Are TV programmers currently doing a satisfactory job of using good taste in curbing excessive violence?

Chart their responses and graph your results on a circle graph on another piece of paper. Be certain to label each portion of the pie. Share your results with the rest of the class and graph the "class results" on the chalkboard.

PROTECTING OURSELVES

When the colonists first came to this country they had guns. They used them for hunting and to protect themselves and their families. There were no policemen around to enforce the laws and prevent violence. Most people lived in the woods, far apart from each other. They depended on their guns for survival. When the time came for them to band together to fight England for their freedom, they formed a militia. Again their guns became very important in fending off the attacks by British soldiers. They eventually won their freedom from England, with a large share of the credit due to their having and knowing how to use firearms.

When the war was over, Americans didn't need guns as much. But the new country was still wild enough for the people to feel that they had a right to own and use their own guns. When the Bill of Rights was added to the Constitution in 1792, the Second Amendment provided for allowance for each state to have its own militia.

But we know that throughout the course of history, guns have been used thousands of times to aid in the successful committing of many violent crimes. There is a constant wave of pressure to make it more difficult to buy and use them.

Much legislation has been passed to control the use of guns. So it's not quite as easy to get a gun as it was many years ago. But there's still a cry among many nonowners of guns for even tighter controls. On the other side, the National Rifle Association and many civil rights groups apply pressure to lessen the controls. The issue remains one of hot controversy.

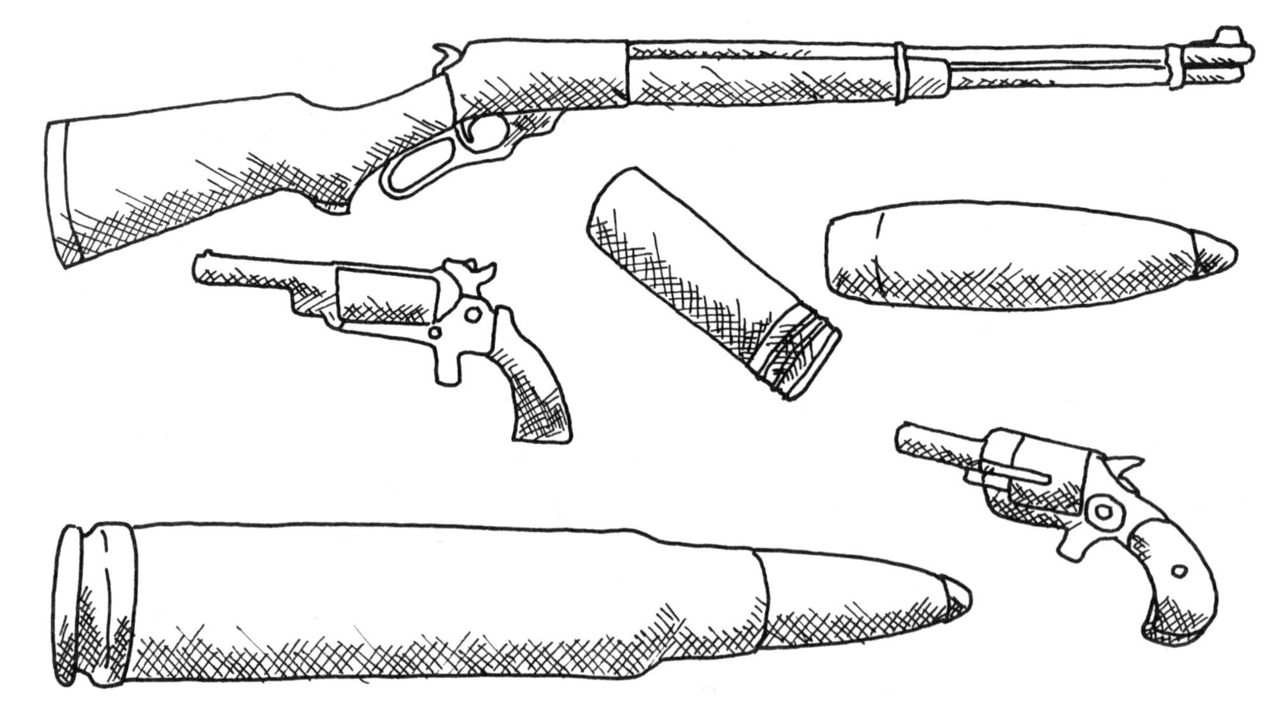

Name ____________________

PROTECTING OURSELVES

1. Find out what the law really says where you live concerning the ownership of firearms. List the rules as they apply to buying a gun, then those which apply to carrying and using one.

2. Statistics often point out that much less violent crime would occur in America if private individuals were not allowed to own firearms. If we are to believe that this is true, why not just ban the future sale of all guns and require people to surrender those they now own.

3. Many cases in court center around the right of an individual to use his weapon to defend himself and oftentimes the decision goes to the victim, even though he may have been attempting to commit a crime. What do you think should be the rules in the use of firearms to defend ourselves? Is taking away those privileges a violation of our own rights in a democracy?

4. Disregarding the crime statistics, we also hear of many accidents every year where innocent victims are maimed or die as a result of accidents involving guns. What are your own opinions about the right to own a gun? Do you own one now? Will you ever own a gun? What good do guns serve?

THE RIGHT TO PRIVACY

Our Constitution guarantees to us all the right to our own privacy. This applies to our homes, our important papers, and to our own selves. While it is sometimes necessary for the police to search people and their belongings to aid them in enforcing the laws, even then there are limitations placed on the search they make. To initiate such a search requires a warrant that has been signed by a judge. The warrant must contain a description of the area to be searched and what it is the officers expect to find. When the search is actually taking place, only those areas specifically listed may be searched.

There are, however, some occasions when the police may act without a warrant. If there is strong suspicion that a crime is in progress, the courts have determined it a matter of common sense for officers upholding the law to step in and stop the crime being committed. But the fine line defining this is sometimes questionable, and a lot of court cases have been dropped by the prosecution because the police had initiated an improper search. Read each situation that follows and decide what you think the fine line of the law should be. Exchange your views with other members of your class.

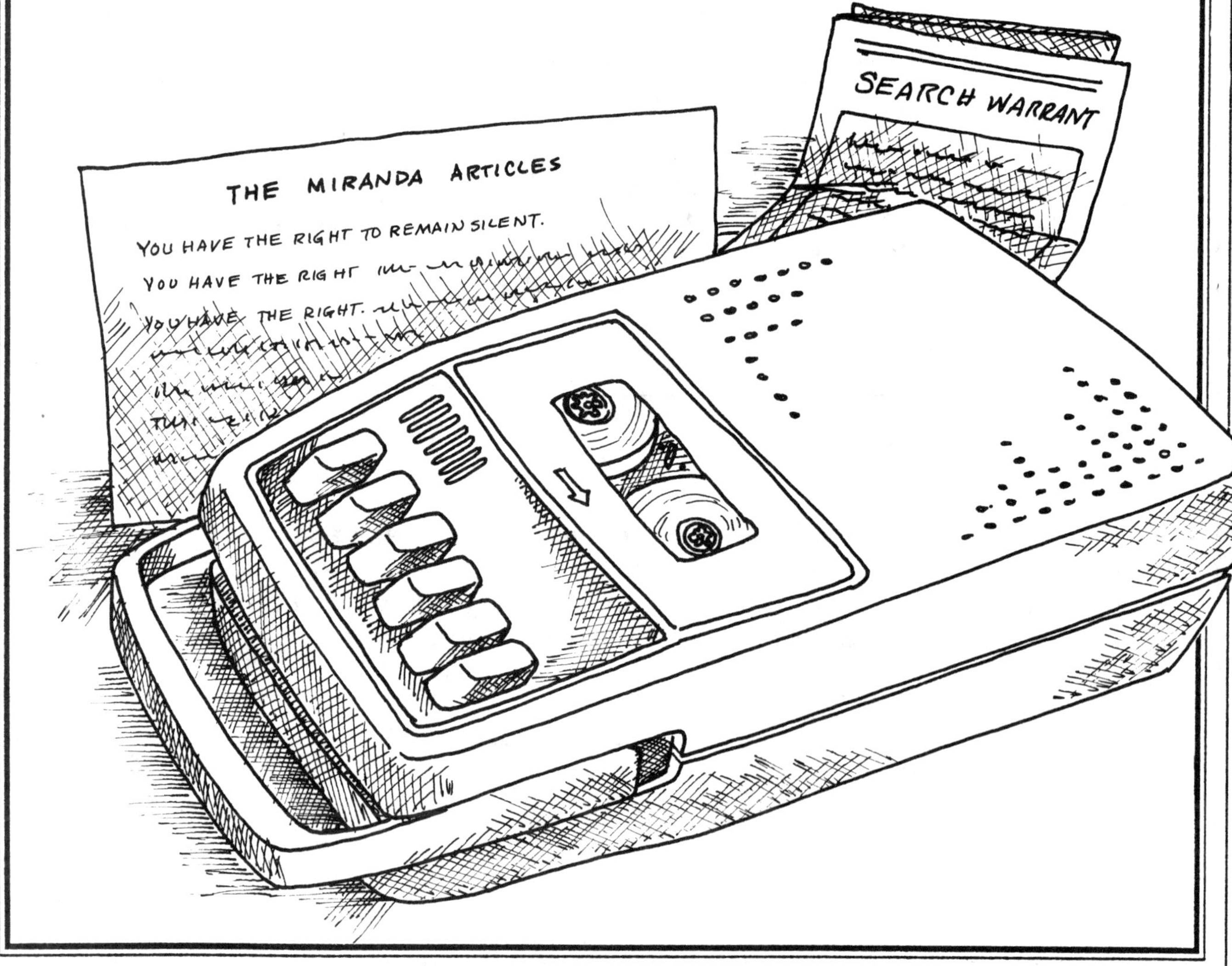

Name ______________________

THE RIGHT TO PRIVACY

Randy Meechum was employed by the Acmar Corporation in the capacity of its chief fiscal officer. Meechum and the other employees at Acmar were unaware that all outgoing calls were monitored and taped as a security precaution. As time passed, it became clear that Meechum was deeply involved in an operation that was not only unethical, but illegal. His mishandling of Acmar funds placed him not only in danger of losing his job, but he could face a term in prison. Can the evidence against Meechum (the tapes) be used by Acmar officials to fire him from his job? Can the tapes be used by the prosecution in its case before the grand jury? Or was the gathering of such evidence against Meechum a violation of his rights to privacy under the Fourth Amendment to the Constitution?

Mr. Bentley, principal of Roosevelt Middle School, has a strong suspicion that Bobby Ray Taylor is dealing in drugs. His suspicions are grounded on a conversation he had with two students who reported that Bobby was selling "pills and marijuana" on school property. Mr. Bentley would like to confront Bobby Ray, but the two students who reported the incident insist on remaining anonymous. They don't want to be labeled snitches. Thus, Mr. Bentley will be on his own when he talks to Bobby Ray. Since the alleged "sale" took place just today during lunch hour, Mr. Bentley figures he better "strike while the iron is hot." His plans are to call Bobby into his office, ask him if he has anything to say about the matter, then escort him to his locker where he will initiate a thorough locker search. Does Mr. Bentley have a right to confront Bobby Ray? Is it right to accuse him of the illegal sale of drugs without divulging the names of the "witnesses"? Does Mr. Bentley have a right to search Bobby's locker without Bobby's permission?

RIGHTS OF THE ACCUSED

The men who wrote the Constitution felt very strongly that living in a democracy should include provisions for protecting those accused of committing crimes until they have been determined to be guilty. Under English rule, many innocent colonists had been banished under the pretense that they had committed criminal acts, when in reality, all they had done was speak out against the harsh rule of the king.

The Fifth Amendment outlines the rights of those accused of breaking the law. The basic premise is that no one should be accused without good reason. There are rules of procedure which authorities must follow that will protect the accused from harrassment and unnecessary harm. Read the text of the Fifth Amendment and then point out the right of the individual covered by that amendment in each of the situations on the following page.

RIGHTS OF THE ACCUSED

Name ______________________

1. Kelly Holmes has been arrested by the police for the murder of her former husband. In taking her off to jail, one of the officers remarks, "She is the only logical choice. I'd say we've probably got ourselves the right suspect here!" Kelly is terrified as she is indeed innocent, but afraid that she is going to jail just because of her past association with her husband. She calms herself somewhat in knowing that she has an alibi for her whereabouts at the time of the murder, . . but "will the police believe me?"

2. Joshua Robinson is accused of robbing the Henry County Savings and Loan of over $40,000 in a late afternoon "stickup." As the evidence of the case unfolds in court, the members of the jury are swayed toward a decision of "not guilty" for lack of convincing evidence against Robinson. Elated with the decision, Josh whispers to his friend as he leaves the courtroom, "Ya-hoo! I got away with one here, but there's nothing they can do about it now!"

3. Monica Lewis makes a decision to testify on her own behalf, because she feels like her own attorney can ask her questions that will convince the jury that she had no part in the murder of Barbara Woods (of which she has been accused). On the other hand, the rules of the court allow the prosecution to cross-examine her because she has chosen to testify. When it comes to the first pointed question by the prosecution, Monica answers, "I refuse to answer that question on the grounds that answering it may tend to incriminate me." She answers other questions in much the same manner.

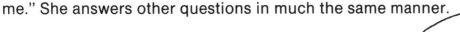

Name ______________________

BARDEE'S QUIK STOP

Bardee's Quik Stop recently opened its doors just across the street from Billy's Place, a long established popular lunch stop at a busy intersection of two major highways. Billy resented the construction of the new fast food restaurant because he knew it would cut into his business. In fact, he did everything he could to stop it, including an attempt to sway the zoning board. But Bardee's is a big chain of fast food restaurants and had a lot of money to back the construction of its new facility, which was elaborate (by fast food standards) and much nicer than Billy's.

Exactly eight days after Bardee's opened it was damaged by fire. Ann Wellborn, sister-in-law of Bardee's owner, Harlan Morris, reported to police that she saw Billy Kibby (owner of Billy's) "fooling around behind Bardee's shortly after midnight" about two hours before the fire started. "He looked like he had something to hide, if you ask me," she said to the police. When the police questioned Billy, he told them that he had gone with Marshall Bradley to a neighboring town to "discuss a business proposition" shortly after he closed Billy's Place at 10:00. Police then talked with Marshall Bradley, but he said he didn't want to get involved. Shortly thereafter, Billy Kibby was arrested on suspicion of starting the fire. He has been indicted by the grand jury and now awaits trial.

Based upon your findings in the Sixth Amendment to the U.S. Constitution, answer the following questions concerning the rights of Billy Kibby:

1. Billy has most of his money tied up in a recent "expansion-remodeling" effort in an attempt to make Billy's Place more attractive to his customers. What does the Constitution say about his rights to a lawyer even if he doesn't have a lot of ready cash available?

____

Name ______________________

BARDEE'S QUIK STOP

2. Even though Billy's dealings with Marshall Bradley may have been somewhat beyond the law (they were actually out smoking marijuana), Marshall represents a legitimate alibi for Billy. What rights does he have regarding this incident when it's perfectly clear why Marshall didn't want to get involved?

____

____

3. If we are to assume that Billy is telling the truth (which he is), then Ann Wellborn is obviously lying. She has very clearly told police that there is no possibility that she could have mistaken Billy for someone else. "It was him for sure!" she said. What rights does Billy have regarding her story?

____

____

4. Place yourself in the shoes of Billy Kibby. You live in a democratic country where this sort of thing just isn't supposed to happen! You are indeed innocent, but things are looking bleak right now. You've been indicted and are going to be forced to the test of a trial, and the evidence strongly suggests that you may be "railroaded" into prison. What course of action would you follow to attempt to make the system work and prove your innocence?

____

____

FINIAS BUTCHER'S LAND

Finias Butcher has lived on his land all of his seventy-one years. His son Simon and his family live on part of the land, too. Before Finias, his father Tillis owned it and before him, his Grandpa Willis. In fact, the land was bought by one of the Butchers from the U.S. Government many years ago when it was nothing more than a government territory. It has passed from one generation to the next ever since. There is indeed a proud tradition here. All of the Butchers were and are farmers. Finias was a little nervous a few years back when he heard talk of making the land a part of a national park. "The beautiful lakes and rolling hills are a natural," the article said. But Finias didn't worry too much. After all, he lived in "America. . . land of the free. . . where a man could do pretty much what he wanted to—a real democracy."

When two people representing the government called on Finias to ask him how much he wanted for his land, he politely told them it wasn't for sale. The next time someone called, Finias was served with an official-looking document which said Finias would have to sell his property under the government's right of *eminent domain*. It even had an appraisal figure telling Finias what the government intended to pay him for his land. This time Finias wasn't so polite. In no uncertain terms he told them to get off his land or he would "go fetch his pellet gun!"

We all know that living in a democracy entitles us to certain rights and freedoms not enjoyed in other more restrictive societies. We also know that a democratic society makes its rules for the benefit of all people. Sometimes some individuals are hurt as a result of those rules that were made to serve the entire society and not the special interests of certain groups and private individuals.

Name ______________________________

FINIAS BUTCHER'S LAND

1. Find the meaning of *eminent domain*, and briefly describe below what it will mean to Finias Butcher and the proud tradition of land ownership that has been passed on for so many generations.

2. What recourse does Finias have at this point? Is there anything he can do, or must he stand helplessly by and be the cause of the break in the Butcher tradition of land ownership?

3. Should he be content with the price offered him in the appraisal, which he says is "grossly unfair," considering that he doesn't want to sell the land anyway? What course of action do you suggest Finias follow at this point?

Name ______________________

FINIAS BUTCHER'S LAND

4. Just how far can eminent domain go? Are we to interpret this to mean that anytime any agency or arm of the government—be it national, state or local—wants any part or all of our property that we must buckle under and give in? This certainly doesn't sound like a democracy. Explain your own thoughts about eminent domain. Should the government have such a right? Present arguments to support your conclusion.

____

____

____

____

____

____

5. We should recognize that eminent domain is one of those necessary rules that exists for the benefit of us all. Look at the list of "proposed" reasons for exercising eminent domain. If you agree that the government should have the right to take the land owned by a private individual, place *yes* in the blank space provided. If you disagree and feel the individual should be justified in keeping his land, write *no* in the space.

YELLOWSTONE

___National Park
___Shopping Mall
___State Park
___Cemetery
___County Jail
___Nuclear Missile Launching Station
___Research Laboratory
___Interstate Highway
___Hospital
___School
___State Highway
___City Landfill
___Water Treatment Facility
___Federal Government Low Income Housing Units

Go back over the list and rank order your choices from the most justifiable to the least justifiable cause for the government's taking the land of a private individual. Then discuss your reasons for your choices in the blank space provided.

____

____

____

Name ______________________________

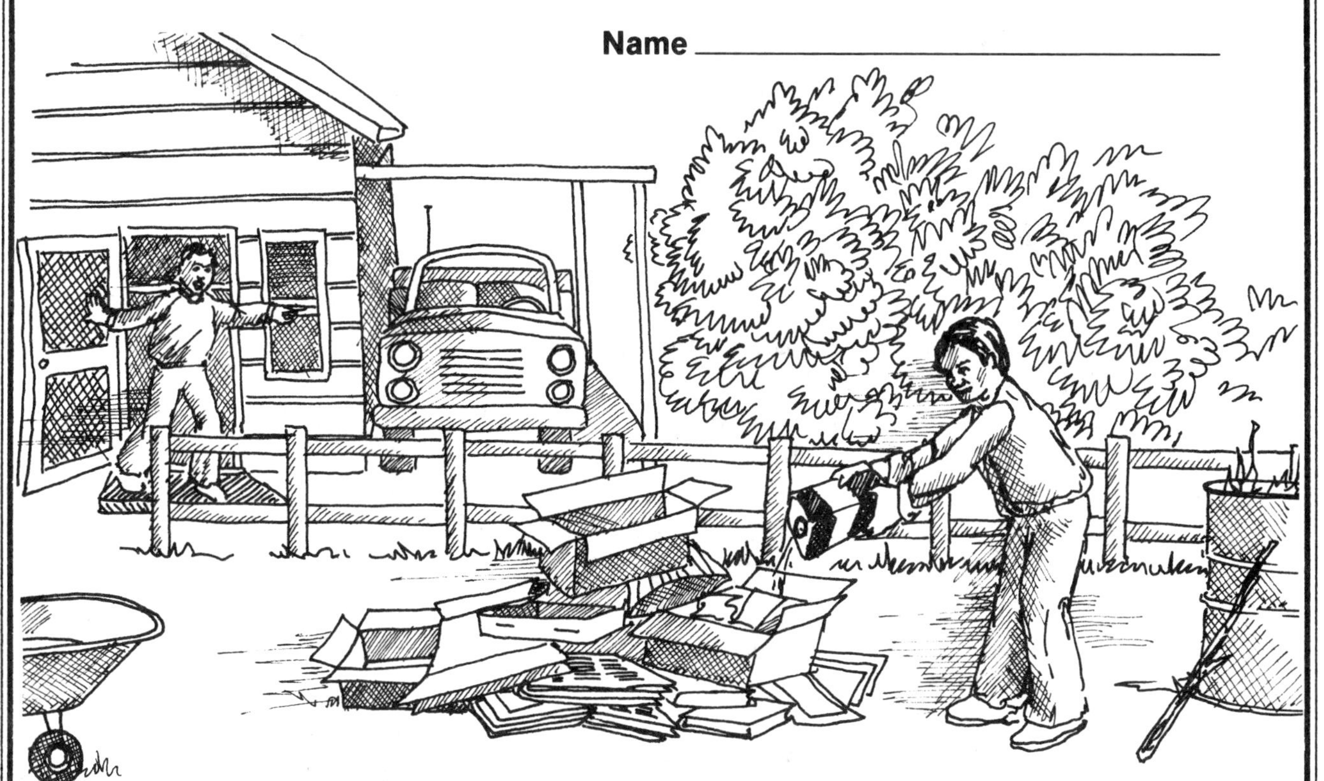

MR. BURNS VS. MR. GREEN

Mr. Burns recently moved to Prophetstown, where he has a new job and has already met several people he can call friends. Yesterday evening he was observed removing several boxes and packing material from his garage, which was accumulated during the course of his family's unpacking. He methodically took them all to his backyard to a point very near the property line that divides his land from Mr. Green's. He then lit a match and stood by while he watched it burn. Mr. Green came roaring out of his house and apprised Mr. Burns in no uncertain terms of the city ordinance in Prophetstown forbidding the burning of trash within the city limits. Mr. Burns responded by saying that he had ". . .burned his trash in Elvaston whenever he wanted. . . and that he didn't know anything about any such ordinance. . . and that until he had some kind of official word, he would continue to burn his trash."

What is your reaction to Mr. Burns' statement? Does the fact that he has no knowledge of the ordinance give him the right to violate the law by burning his trash? What would you do if you were Mr. Green? He has clearly pointed out the law to Mr. Burns, and it's quite evident that he is upset by the smoke that is wafting through his house. What advice, if any, do you have for Mr. Burns?

____

____

____

____

____

MANDATORY DRUG TESTING

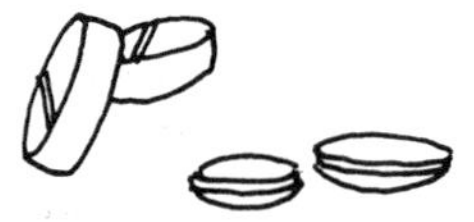

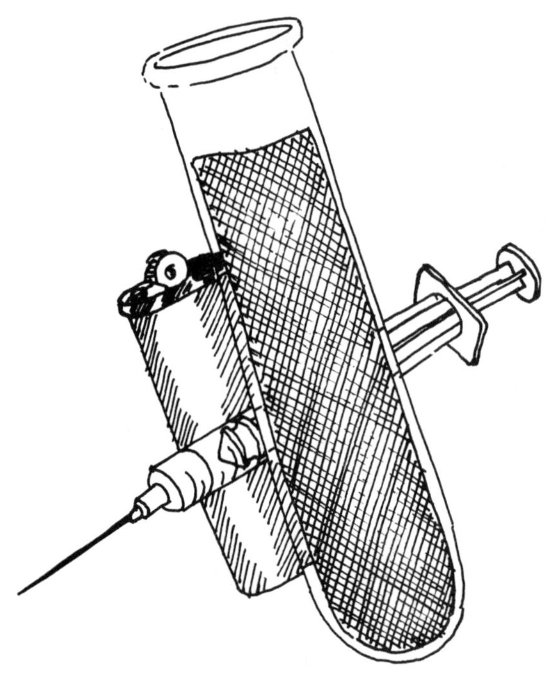

Drug use has become a major concern in the United States during the past few years. More recently the spread of the deadly disease AIDS has brought lawmakers to come to grips with the problem. The result has been that many businesses make it a matter of policy to require mandatory drug testing for their employees. These tests can evaluate a number of different chemicals in the blood, including past drug use and disease. The main objectives of such testing are to stop the spread of dangerous diseases and to reduce drug and alcohol abuse, which have become serious problems for employers.

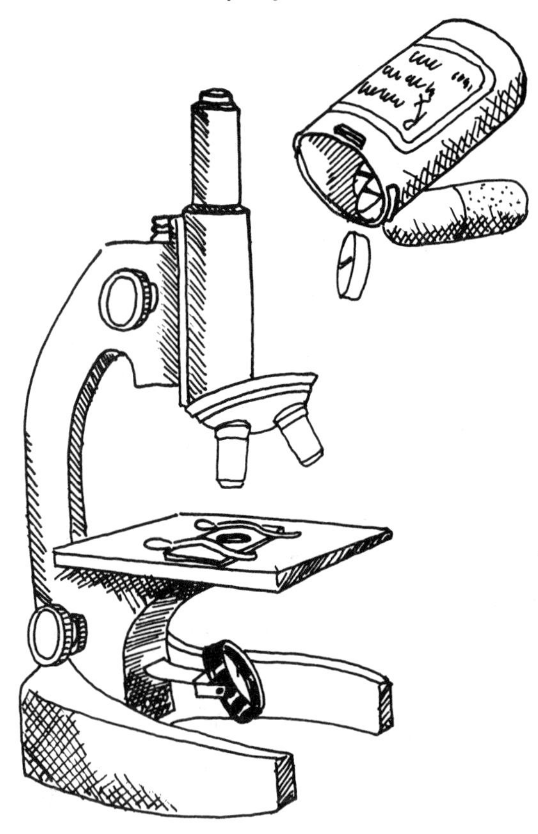

While the objectives of such tests are certainly legitimate cause for their existence, they nonetheless raise certain questions. First, such tests are not always accurate. Mistakes are sometimes made. It's also possible for people to cheat on blood and urine tests unless they are closely monitored. Another potential problem stems from the fact that some drugs can remain in a person's system for a long time. To label an individual as a drug user and to deny him a job on the basis of a single foolish act committed long ago really wouldn't be very fair. Finally, any such mandatory testing must be considered an invasion of the personal rights we all have come to cherish.

Name ______________________

MANDATORY DRUG TESTING

1. The advocates of mandatory testing insist, however, that all benefits outweigh the potential harm. It has often been said that the answer to America's drug problem lies in eliminating the supply. In a recent year the Air Force spent $45.6 million to catch planes used to smuggle drugs into this country. The result was two drug busts. The Navy spent over $37 million and seized twenty drug-carrying vessels. The Army spent over $8 million and would not release figures. Despite such failure, there are calls for increased use of the military to combat the drug problem. What is your reaction to these statistics? Is this the answer to our war on drugs, or do you have other suggestions?

2. If we take a close look at the market for illegal drugs in this country, we see an almost perfect example of a well-functioning capitalistic market. The laws of supply and demand are in complete control. Demand creates the direction of the markets. If there are people willing to pay, there is encouragement to others to provide a supply. Decreasing the supply only drives up the price and encourages new suppliers to become involved in drug traffic. Such laws of supply and demand lie at the very heart of this democratic society in which we live. But we all know the danger of using drugs. How then can you relate your thoughts on solving the drug problem (from question #1) to fit the laws of a capitalistic society? What do we do to solve our nation's drug problem?

Name ______________________________

HOW FAR DO WE GO?

A politician recently said of mandatory drug testing: "It (mandatory testing) is definitely in the wave of the future. Because of the serious problems we now have with illegal drugs in this country, you're going to see more and more mandatory drug testing. This may be in part a solution to our drug abuse problem. But at what expense? Each time this happens and the people are forced to subject themselves to drug testing, those involved will be a little bit less free than they were before." What are your own opinions about the limits to such mandatory drug tests? To ensure that people don't cheat on drug tests, they are sometimes forced into some humiliating situations one would not expect to find in this democratic country. How far can the government (and private industry) go in the war on drugs before they are infringing on the precious rights of the people?

____

____

____

____

____

____

____

Mandatory drug testing certainly does not affect all people in all jobs. Who should be tested? When is it important and when does it not matter? Or, perhaps you think everyone applying for a job should be tested. What is your opinion?

____

____

____

____

____

____

____

____

____

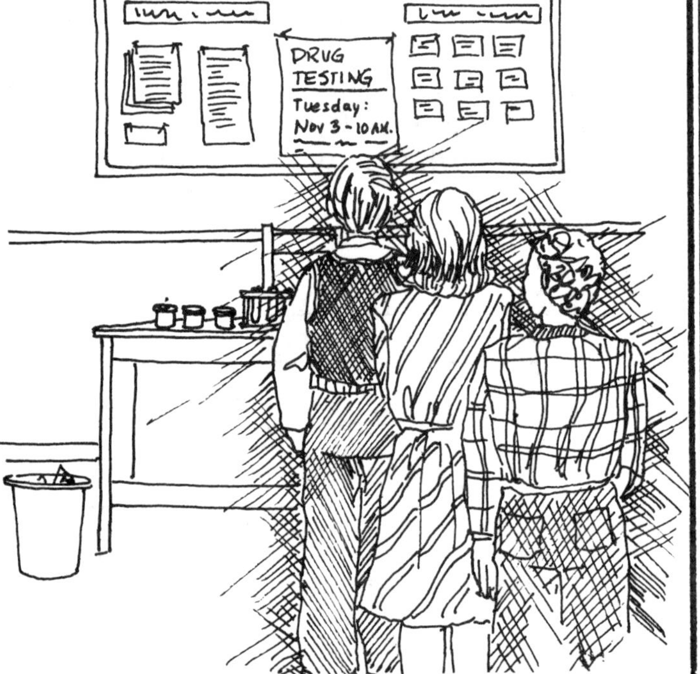

Name ______________________

ALBERT THOMAS' TICKET

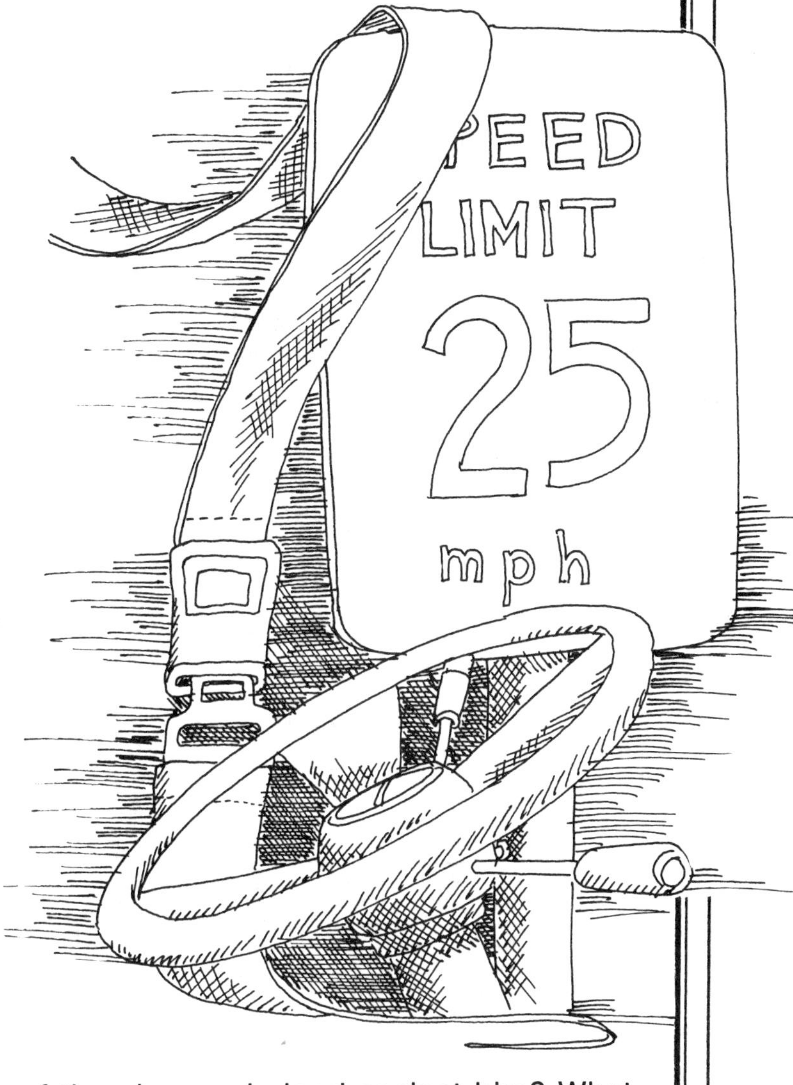

Albert Thomas was recently cited by police for speeding, improper lane usage and not having his seat belt on when police pulled him over. The arresting officer informed Albert that he had been clocked with a police radar gun at 48 miles per hour in a 25 mph speed zone. Albert responded to this statement by saying he had "driven this same road for five years and never noticed any posted speed limits anywhere." The officer then told Albert about the location points of the posted speed limits; but Albert simply said, "I didn't see them. . . ,but even if they're there, 25 mph is ridiculous!" The officer then cited Albert for passing a motorist (at about the same time he went through the radar) in a no passing zone. Albert had an answer here, too: "That stupid idiot in front of me was going so slow, it was either pass him or run over him!" Finally, on the matter of Albert's failure to be "buckled up," he simply said, "It's been broken for a long time. I'll get it fixed if you want me to. But don't be giving me any tickets. I'm short on cash right now, and I've got a lot of bills to pay."

Does Albert have any recourse on any of the charges lodged against him? What is wrong with his logic in each of the arguments he used for breaking the law? What are Albert's responsibilities as a driver? If you were the arresting officer, how would you handle the above situation? Do you have any advice for Albert Thomas?

____

____

____

____

____

____

Name ______________________

LOCAL LAWS

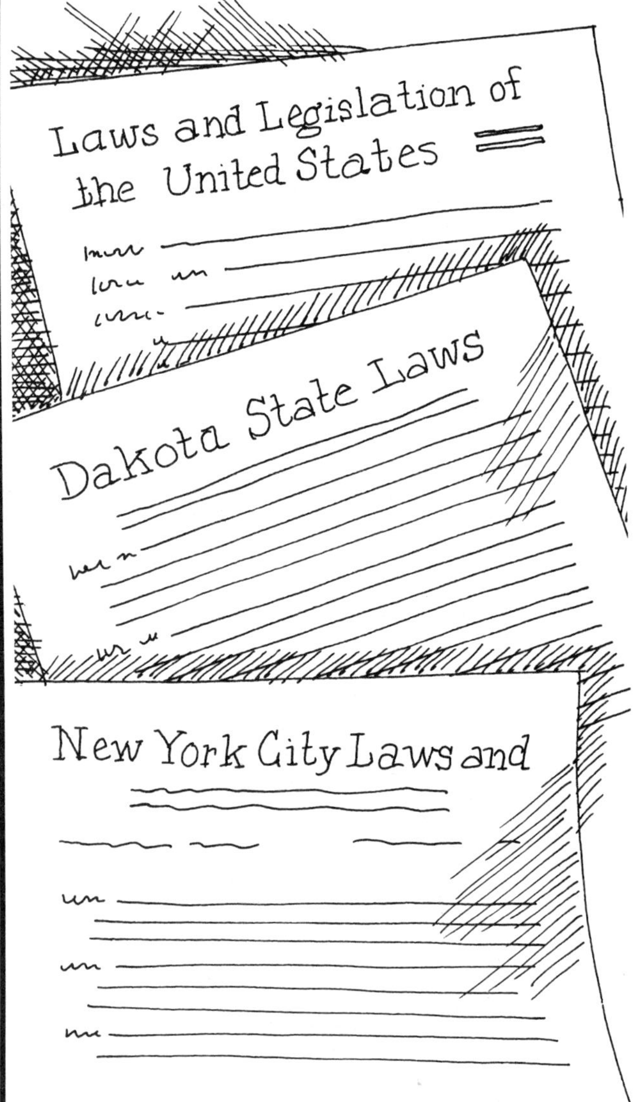

Societies must have rules and laws to control the actions of those who have little regard for the welfare of others. There are laws at the national level that are made to affect everyone for the good of the nation. There are laws made at the state level that are passed to limit and control the behavior of the citizens of that state as well as travelers and visitors who are passing through. And then there are local rules and laws that apply specifically to the community in which they exist.

A state law can never be in conflict with an existing national law, and local laws can neither be in conflict with state or national laws. But there are special situations in each state where it is important for the legislators of that state to decide exactly what is in the best interest of the people of that state. So state laws can vary from one state to another. When we get down to the local level, there are even more special interests and situations that can best be resolved by making local rules that will best serve the members of that community.

1. If we have a single list of rules and laws at the national level (which apply to all of us), why is it necessary for each state and, in turn, each community to have its own set of rules that apply at the state and then the local level?

____

____

____

2. What factors would probably help to shape the framework of rule making at the local level?

____

____

____

Name ______________________

LOCAL LAWS

3. List three national laws that apply to all of us.

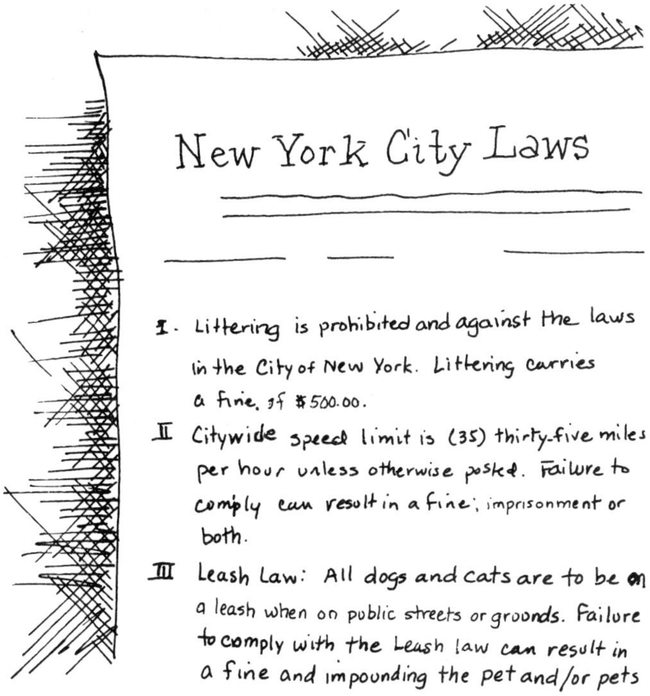

New York City Laws

I. Littering is prohibited and against the laws in the City of New York. Littering carries a fine of $500.00.

II Citywide speed limit is (35) thirty-five miles per hour unless otherwise posted. Failure to comply can result in a fine, imprisonment or both.

III Leash Law: All dogs and cats are to be on a leash when on public streets or grounds. Failure to comply with the Leash law can result in a fine and impounding the pet and/or pets

4. List three state laws that apply to the citizens of your state and those who are visiting.

5. List three local laws or rules that apply to residents of your community.

6. When it comes to making rules and laws, which level—national, state or local—comes closest to "pure democracy"?

Name______________________________

LOCAL LEADERS

The first step in the electoral process is to determine who gets to vote. Even those who are native-born United States citizens must meet certain requirements to make them eligible to vote. Find out the qualifications necessary for the local representatives where you live. After listing those qualifications, place a star(*) beside those you've already satisfied.

____

____

____

____

Once a potential voter qualifies by meeting the established criteria, the final step is to actually register. Once voting registration has occurred, the voter has the right to vote. However, simply having the right to vote does not necessarily make a voter a good one. What responsibilities can you think of that go hand in hand with properly serving the democratic process?

____

____

____

____

Who are your local leaders? After naming each, indicate his/her political party. Then indicate the term of office for each of these local leaders.

Mayor______________________________

____

Sheriff (or Police Chief) ______________________________

____

Alderman ______________________________

____

Others ______________________________

____

What properly qualifies those who serve in each of these capacities? Does any of these jobs require special training or education? Should there be additional requirements to properly fulfill the demands of these jobs?

____

____

____

____

Name ______________________________

LOCAL SERVICES

The communities in which we live provide for us a number of services that make our lives better and more convenient. Since these services are performed by people who depend on their jobs for their livelihood, they cost money. Rather than charging for them on an individual basis, they are paid for by the taxes levied against those who live in the community. Such services usually fall within these four major groups: safety, health, education or recreation. Below is an example of each. Write under each picture the group classification to which each belongs.

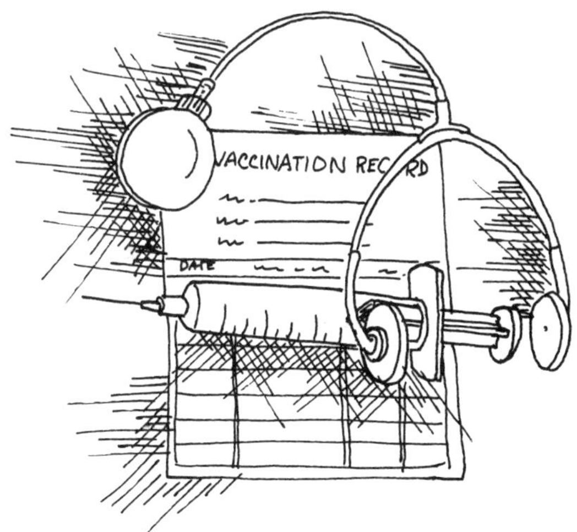

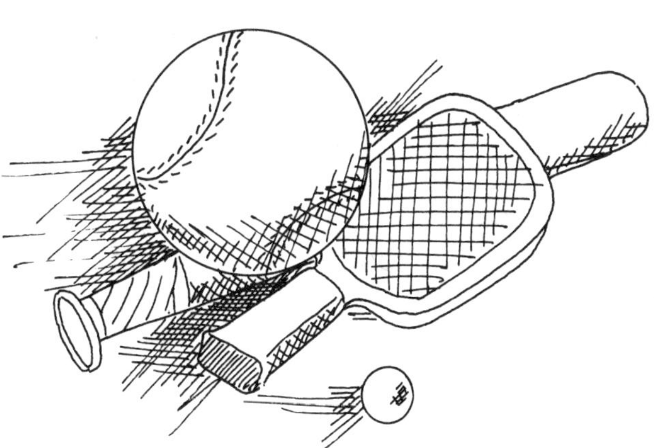

Find out about other services that are available in your community. List each worker under the heading that best classifies the type of service performed.

Name ____________________

LOCAL SERVICES

What two factors determine the services that are available to a community?

____

____

____

____

If your answer to the last question was the size of the city and the amount of money available to pay for services, your answer was correct. Obviously a large city would have a greater need for more of these services as well as more money to pay for them. But there's often a catch there, too. Paying for services like fire and police protection and education requires a lot of money. And the more people. . . the more fire and police protection and the more teachers needed to cover more classrooms. Hence, more money is needed to pay for these services.

Where does the money come from? You learned earlier that tax dollars are largely responsible for paying for such services. While there are several different kinds of taxes levied to provide additional revenue, taxes assessed against property owners is one of the more important ones. Unfortunately, many of our nation's large cities have many poor people. They either don't own property at all or if they do, its value is so low that it doesn't provide much of a tax base for collecting revenue. But the people themselves are still there and they need the health care and protection and education we've been talking about.

1. Research the source of funds used to run your city or community. Where does the money come from? How much does it cost to run your city for an entire year?

   ____

   ____

   What services do you and other members of your community get for your money?

   ____

   ____

Name ______________________

LOCAL SERVICES

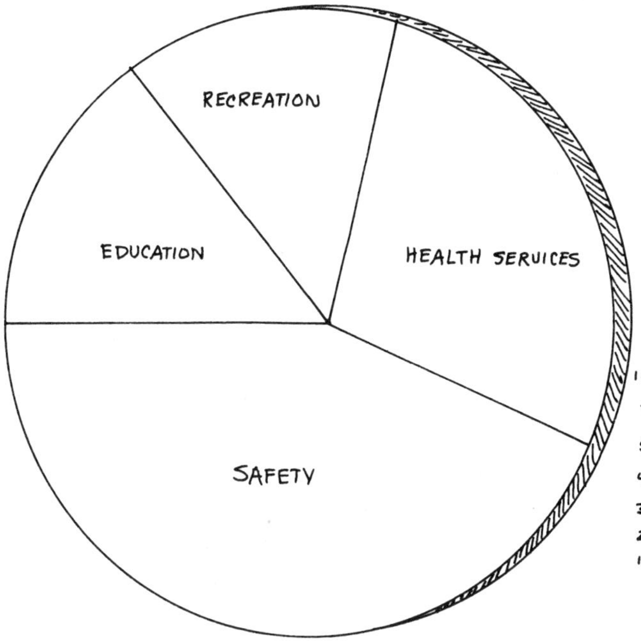

RECREATION

EDUCATION

HEALTH SERVICES

SAFETY

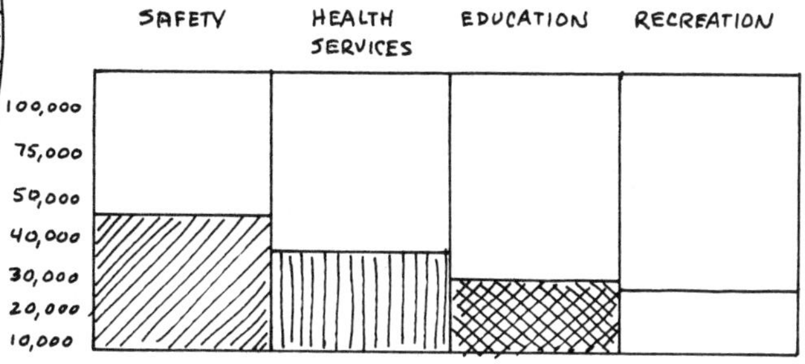

	SAFETY	HEALTH SERVICES	EDUCATION	RECREATION
100,000				
75,000				
50,000				
40,000				
30,000				
20,000				
10,000				

2. It is often helpful to portray such figures in the form of a circle graph, showing the public how each dollar is spent. Most governing city lawmakers also show the people where the money comes from. Show this graphically as well as presenting the results of your findings.

Where the money comes from. . .

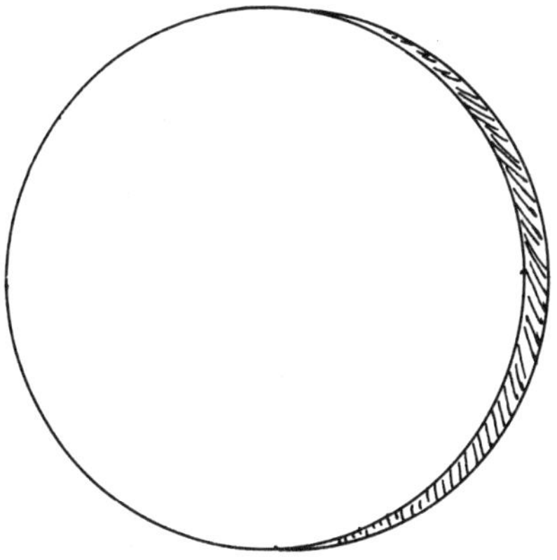

Where the money goes. . .

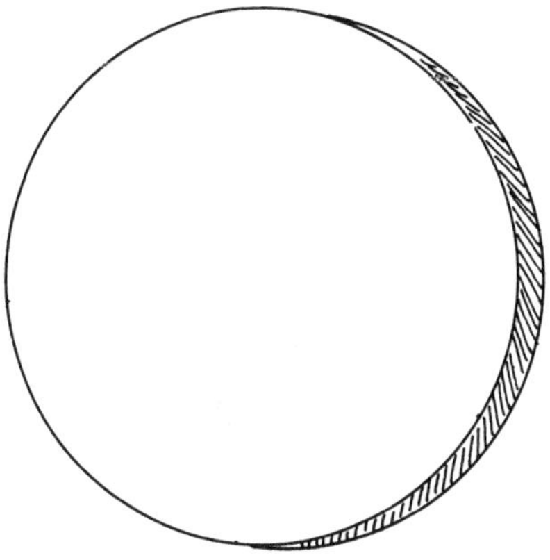

Name ____________________________

THE PEOPLE SPEAK OUT

While many of our laws are made at the federal level, there are laws made to govern each state and each local community. Those laws are made by the state and local lawmakers. But beyond that, the people themselves have a right to step forward and be heard when it comes to making laws. The powers described below serve as a check by the people on the lawmakers who make our laws, both at the state and local levels.

Referendum

First there is the power of *referendum*. This check on lawmakers by the people is used in most states whenever raising money is the issue. At the local level, its most common use centers around school boards wanting additional money to finance the ever-increasing costs of education. That money more often than not will come from the taxpayer in the form of higher property taxes. So the school boards place the issues before the people and let them decide. Are they willing to pay more for education or not? It's often that simple. It then becomes a matter of the strong advocates of each position trying to influence the voting public before the actual referendum takes place.

Initiative

The power of *initiative* involves the voters themselves creating the idea for a change in the law. Once the change has been refined into its most concise and presentable format, signatures are sought to lend it support. In most states five to ten percent of that state's voters are needed to support an idea to get it placed before the general voting public. Once that support is achieved, the proposed change becomes a referendum for all the people affected to decide. The power of initiative is often referred to as a grass roots form of government, because the idea started at the very bottom with the people themselves.

Recall

The power of *recall* is reserved for the people as a way of removing from office an elected official for failing to do his job properly. Terms of office usually extend for a specific number of years. If the citizens feel that an official is doing an unsatisfactory job in performing his duties, they can demand that a referendum be presented to all of the voting public to decide if the official should or should not be allowed to finish his term of office. To do this requires a specific number of signatures as determined by that state's legislature.

Name ______________________________

THE PEOPLE SPEAK OUT

Look at each example below and identify the type of power used by the people in each case.

In California a group of citizens decide that enough is enough! They have been taxed to the point that many people are losing their homes because they can't pay their property taxes. School officials are begging for even more money to meet the escalating costs of education. More money for school means higher property taxes because that is the source of most school funds. The leaders of this protest have taken a stand that property taxes should never exceed one percent of their assessed valuation. Over 25,000 supporters of this position signed their names to petitions that were circulated all over the county. Because this was a significant percentage of all registered voters and qualified under law, the issue was placed on a ballot before the general voting public. The voters overwhelmingly approved the ceiling on property taxes by a vote of nearly 4 to 1. Thus the schools will have to solve their financial woes some other way.

The mayor of a small city has been accused of mishandling over $100,000 in public monies entrusted to him. A grand jury has indicted him on criminal charges, but he has not yet been brought to trial. Thus he remains a free man out on bail. In the best interests of the city, the city council has officially asked him to resign from office. Although the evidence strongly suggests that he is guilty, he contends that the charges are unfair, and he refuses to resign from office. There remains over fourteen months of his term as mayor, and several of the local citizens feel that is too long to wait for another mayor. Many who feel he is guilty fear that he will continue to misuse public funds. To bring the matter to action, a group of "concerned citizens" circulate a petition calling for a test of election among the voters to determine whether or not he should remain in office. Local rules dictate that it takes a three-fifths majority to forcibly remove an elected official before his term expires. The vote is 2176 against his remaining in office and 1012 in favor of his remaining mayor. Therefore he is removed from office.

Search through newspapers and magazines for examples of the powers of individual citizens. Copy or bring to class each article and describe to other students the specific type of power referred to in each article.

Name ____________________

MY STATE GOVERNMENT

Below is a blueprint that follows the lines of authority for most state governments. Find out the information needed to complete the diagram for your state. If the outline doesn't fit your state as it is presented below, change the diagram to correctly show your state's government.

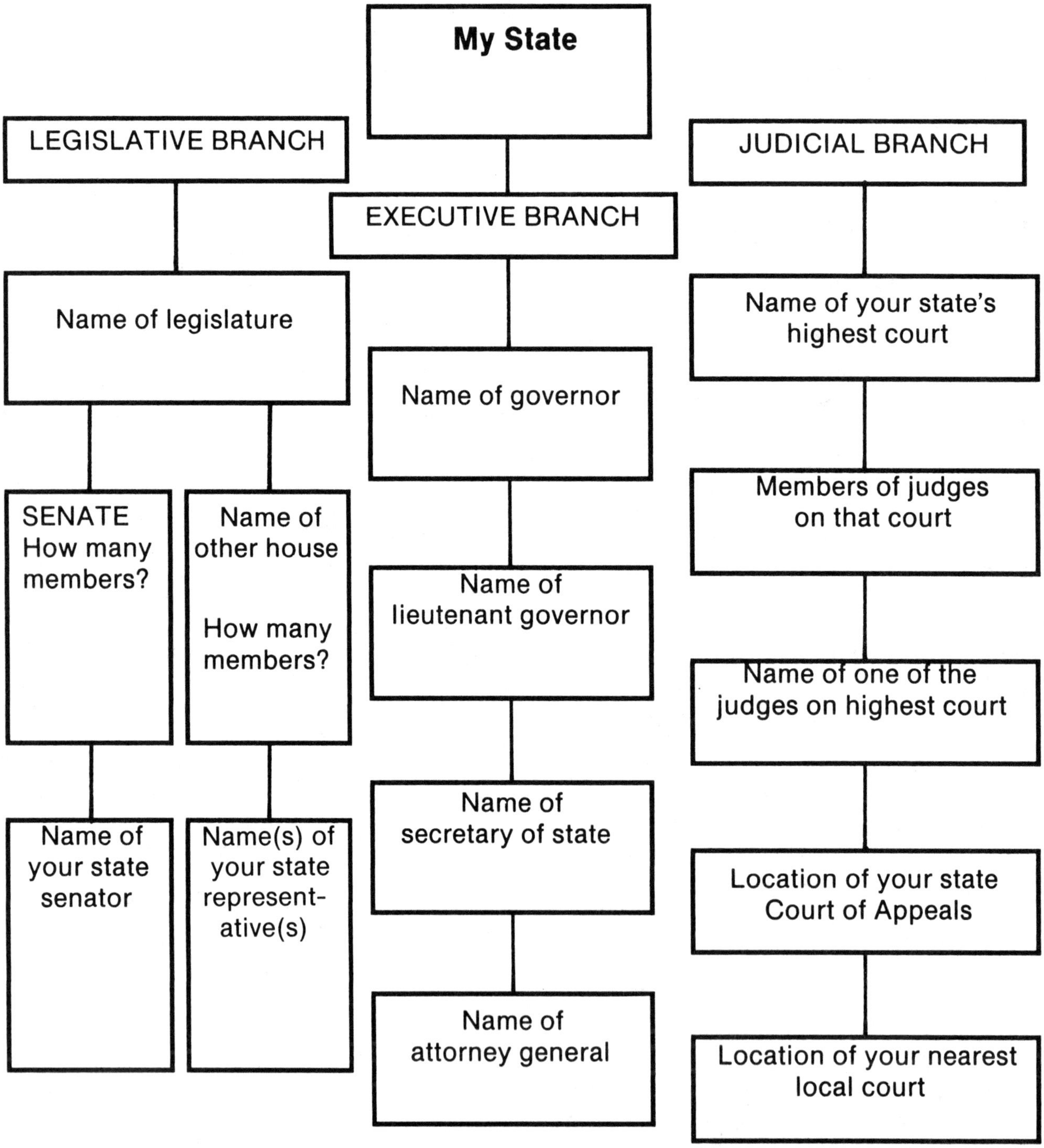

My State

LEGISLATIVE BRANCH

- Name of legislature
  - SENATE How many members?
    - Name of your state senator
  - Name of other house How many members?
    - Name(s) of your state representative(s)

EXECUTIVE BRANCH

- Name of governor
- Name of lieutenant governor
- Name of secretary of state
- Name of attorney general

JUDICIAL BRANCH

- Name of your state's highest court
- Members of judges on that court
- Name of one of the judges on highest court
- Location of your state Court of Appeals
- Location of your nearest local court

EXECUTIVE ORDER 9066

NOW, THEREFORE, by virtue of the authority vested in me as President of the United States and Commander-in-Chief of the Army and Navy, I hereby authorize and direct the Secretary of War, and the Military Commanders whom he may from time to time designate, whenever he or any designated Commander deems such action necessary or desirable, to prescribe military areas in such places and of such extent as he or the appropriate Military Commander may determine, from which any or all persons may be excluded, and with respect to which, the right of any person to enter, remain in, or leave shall be subject to whatever restrictions the Secretary of War or the appropriate Military Commander may impose on his discretion. . . .

Franklin D. Roosevelt
February 19, 1942

It was this executive order that laid the groundwork for the internment of thousands of Japanese-Americans during World War II. When the Japanese shocked the world by bombing Pearl Harbor on December 7, 1941, there arose an almost overnight mass hysteria of distrust against all Japanese living in America. By the spring of 1942, the government had begun the internment of 110,000 of its residents, two thirds of them natural-born Americans. None were ever charged individually with doing anything, but rather it was a collective accusation against all citizens and aliens of Japanese heritage. It was felt by some Americans that the Japanese had been "planted" here to sabotage and undermine the top level secrets of the United States. In answer to the apprehension and fear, General John L. DeWitt, Commander of the Western Defense Command, responded by declaring the states of California, Washington and Oregon as strategic areas and ordered the removal of persons of Japanese ancestry living there. The first such centers were established at Manzunar, California, and Posten, Arizona. Other centers at Tule Lake, California; Gila River, Arizona; Granada, Colorado; Topaz, Utah; Minidoka, Idaho; Jerome, Arkansas; and Heart Mountain, Wyoming, were all created later in some of the most unsavory regions of the United States. The evacuees suffered from extreme cold in the winter and stifling heat in the summer.

The shame of this black mark in American history is indeed one of the incongruities of a nation founded on a basis of freedom, equality and opportunity.

Name ______________________________

EXECUTIVE ORDER 9066

1. A CAUSE FOR SHAME

There was never one single instance proven that a native-born American of Japanese ancestry ever attempted any act of sabotage or disloyalty. In the years after the war, many fair-minded American citizens realized the gross injustices that had been done, but they admitted it quietly. . . because it is fact that history is written by those who live it. What reasons can you think of that would alter the philosophy of a nation that stood for freedom and the personal rights of individuals and resorted to such tactics?

____

____

____

2. DEEP-ROOTED HISTORICAL PREJUDICE

Research the history behind the anti-Japanese movement that was in some ways a continuation of the long-standing feeling against the Chinese that began in the 1850's. After reading about this page in American history, jot down the reasons for the two separate mass migrations of Chinese that set the stage for the resentment against the Japanese when they began arriving in the 1890's.

____

____

____

3. THE INFLUENCE OF THOSE IN COMMAND

Below are direct quotes from people who were in power or newspaper headlines that appeared preceding the internment of Japanese-Americans.

The Japanese race is an enemy race.
Japs Keep Out. . . You Rats!
Californians Seek to Eject All Japs
Treachery, Loyalty to Emperor— Inherent Japanese Traits
Let's get rid of them now!
It takes 8 tons of freight to K.O. 1 Jap.
I'm for deporting them back to Japan.

What responsibilities do people have who hold political offices or run newspapers when it comes to making public their personal feelings? How do such statements lead to innocent victims being harmed by their words? How did such comments victimize the innocent Japanese-Americans?

____

____

____

Name ______________________________

EXECUTIVE ORDER 9066

Divide the class into groups of three to four students each. Group members are to discuss the following simulation:

WHAT IF. . . you lived back in the 1940's next door to a family of Japanese-Americans. The shock of Pearl Harbor greatly troubled all Americans. But what if you had had an older brother serving in the United States Army at the time? How would you feel about the family next door? Discuss how your concern for a member of your family might affect your behavior toward the family next door. After you've talked this through as a group, share with other members of the class how you honestly feel you would have acted? Can you empathize with why some Americans reacted the way they did? What about the family next door?

____

____

____

____

____

____

____

AN ECONOMIC TRAGEDY. . .
The Japanese-Americans also suffered almost incalculable economic losses as a result of their relocation. They were forced to sell their property at a fraction of its value, and opportunists are said to have often been paid less than ten percent of the true market value of their land and possessions. Losses to the Nisei were estimated in the hundreds of millions of dollars. How does allowing this violate the American principles of democracy? What constitutional rights were violated by this action? If the entire incident had happened today, how do you think it would be handled differently? Are minorities better protected today?

____

____

____

____

____

____

____

Name________________________________

THE FEDERAL BUDGET

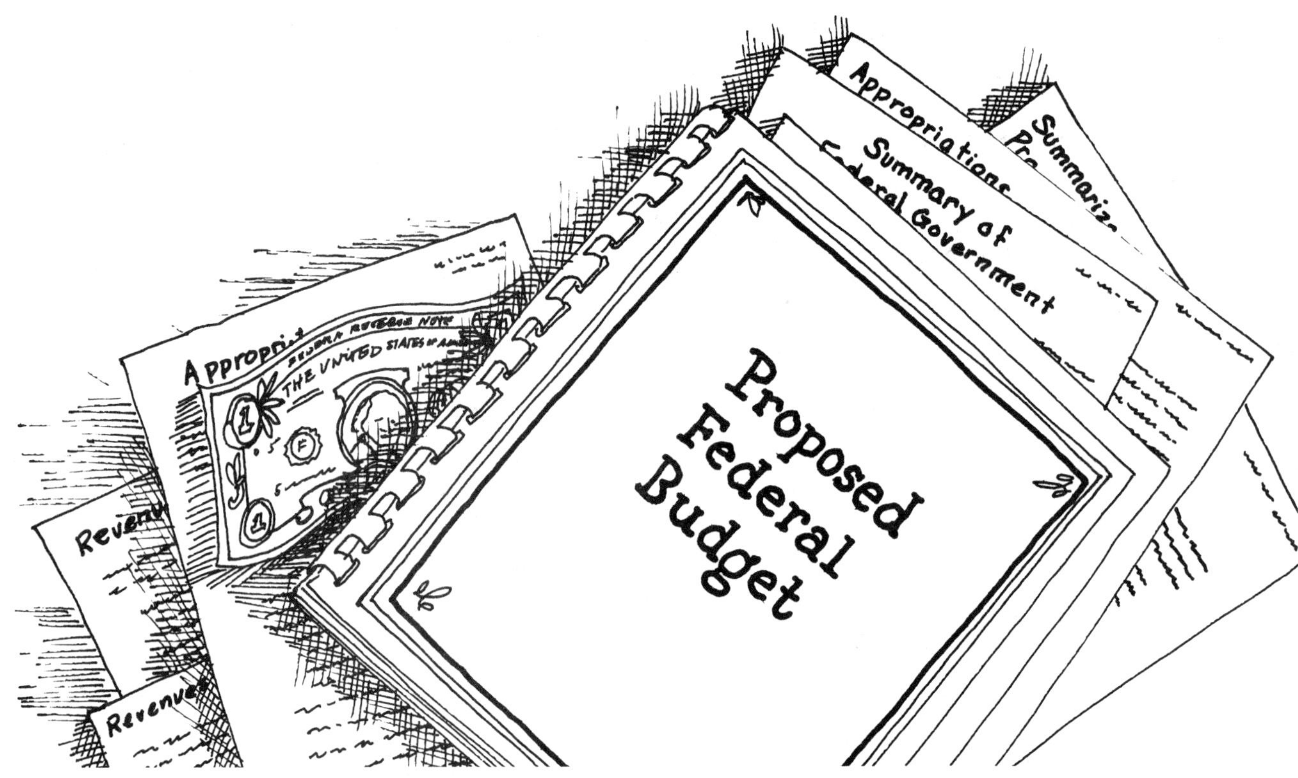

For many years the government has spent more money than it has collected in revenue. It does this because of the huge amount of money required to pay for all the services and subsidies our government provides. Each year the debt continues to rise higher and higher. To keep the government afloat and to keep the continued flow of money going to all the areas in which it has been directed, our government must continue to borrow additional money. This only adds further to the growing national debt. There are some solutions, but none is without its price. Perhaps the simplest solution would be to simply stop spending more than we collect in taxes and other revenue. But the implications of such an idea can be pretty frightening!

If spending is cut, where do the cuts occur? Our largest expense by far is the defense budget. But if cuts are made here, what does that do to our national security? Perhaps our government could cut some of the support to some of the many social and welfare programs it currently sponsors. But which ones? Most of the programs currently being subsidized by our government are still not considered enough by many to really do an adequate job. If spending is cut in specific areas, what happens to the welfare of the victims of those spending cuts?

Another solution to the problems of the nation's financial woes is to raise taxes. However, few politicians openly support tax hikes because of their unpopularity with the voters who select them.

Name ________________________

THE FEDERAL BUDGET

Find out the dollar figure of the most recently approved federal budget for the current fiscal year. Express that figure by writing it out completely numerically.

If the current population of the United States is approximately 200 million, how much would each person have to pay to create a balanced budget?

Find out the dollar extent of the current national debt and write it in the space below.

What are the negative implications of such a staggering figure? What effect do you think this has with respect to other nations around the world?

The problems associated with the federal budget often resemble a cat chasing its tail. The more we spend the greater into debt we become. As the spending continues to rise with inflation just to maintain a consistent level of services to the people of the United States, the problem becomes even more severe. What possible solutions do you have for this staggering and somewhat overwhelming problem? What are the options? Which of the alternatives do you favor?

OUR NATION'S DEFENSE

Each year the Congressmen and women we elect to make our laws authorize the spending of billions of dollars to ensure our safety against attack by others. Many people often criticize such spending because they say we have all the sophisticated weapons we need to defend ourselves properly against an attack by an unfriendly nation. The Soviet Union has long been our chief rival in world affairs. Since the 1950's, the two nations have continued to create even more destructive weapons to protect themselves and their allies from each other. Even though we now have very sophisticated weaponry that could be activated in a matter of seconds, we continue to develop technology even further because we are afraid the Soviet Union will create something in the future that will make our weapons obsolete. The Soviet Union employs the same kind of defense strategy.

Where does it all end? Arms control has been discussed by the two nations for many years. Agreements to eliminate some of their missiles have been made. Some of the weapons have been diffused. But there is still a long way to go toward achieving the trust between the two nations necessary to make the arms race a thing of the past.

To complicate the matter further, other countries now have nuclear weapons. The hotbed of trouble in the Middle East has stirred up a great deal of anti-American feelings among some of the people who live there. We must be constantly on the alert against an unwarranted attack.

On the other side of the aisle are those who are calling for major cuts in our defense spending. They point to the domestic problems here at home that could be solved with the billions of dollars spent annually on our nation's defense. Those same people cite the problems of the poor and the homeless and the hungry as being a disgrace in a country as rich as ours.

Name ____________________

OUR NATION'S DEFENSE

So the debate goes on. Those we have elected to make our laws continue to authorize the annual spending of vast sums of money to upgrade our nation's defense. . . but they do so in the name of self-preservation. They insist that our weapons will never be used aggressively against another country.

What is your reaction to the defense budget of the United States? Find out how many dollars of the current fiscal budget are earmarked for defense spending. What percent of the total U.S. budget do they represent? Do you agree with the critics who suggest the money could be better spent elsewhere? If so, what are your priorities? What will happen if we take money from the defense budget? Perhaps you feel we aren't spending enough to protect ourselves against the Soviet Union and other nations who pose a constant threat to the United States. Share your thoughts on this issue and develop what you feel is the best plan for the United States.

FAILING FARMERS

The American farmer is in trouble! For years farmers in the United States produced not only enough food to feed America, but many underdeveloped foreign nations as well. As farming technology improved around the world, those nations formerly dependent upon the American farmer began to produce their own food. Farmers here continued to produce. Prices fell because of the basic laws of supply and demand. A greater supply than is needed (demand) results in a lower price on the market.

The federal government came to the aid of farmers by buying up the surpluses to give some support to falling prices. Low interest loans were also available to farmers. Programs were even established to pay farmers not to produce more crops and dairy products in an effort to keep prices within reason. This support added billions of dollars to the national debt. Many farmers used much of the money they received from the above sources to expand their own operations. They bought additional farmland and expensive equipment and found themselves deep into debt.

To add further to their woe, a severe drought across the Great Plains and the Midwest caused many areas to produce virtually no crops at all. Putting all this together, the result has been that many farmers have lost their land. Thousands more are on the very brink of financial ruin.

Name ______________________

FAILING FARMERS

What are your suggestions for helping the American farmer? Please remember that the dollars you may want to give to them must come from somewhere. . . and that "somewhere" is most likely the American taxpayer. You must also consider that in a democracy there is as little government intervention as possible. Any time the government does become involved, there are usually strings attached.

How do you think the problem of the American farmer would be handled in the Soviet Union?

What are the far-reaching implications down the road ten years from now if the U.S. government does not help the American farmer?

ENVIRONMENTAL CONCERNS

As a nation, the advances we've made in technology that have improved our lives and given us greater convenience have certainly not been without their cost. We are in the midst of trying to save our environment. Nuclear power has proven its value as an abundant future source of energy. But what do we do with the hazardous cancer-causing radioactive waste it leaves behind? Scientists also believe that the waste materials left behind by heavy industry are destroying the ozone layer of the earth's atmosphere. The ozone layer filters out many of the harmful ultraviolet rays of the sun.

Many beautiful beaches that border our nation's coastline and serve as vacation playgrounds have been closed periodically because of raw sewage and other sickening debris that has washed back onto our shores. Pesticides used by farmers have washed into our rivers and streams and have been the cause of the loss of millions of fish annually. Such pollution also presents some rather scary health hazards to the people themselves who drink the water and eat the surviving fish and the cattle who drink from those waters.

Name ____________________

ENVIRONMENTAL CONCERNS

The burning of millions of tons of coal to provide cheap energy for a nation dependent upon industry has sent a residue up into the atmosphere that returns to the earth as an acid rain that destroys vegetation. Just what can be done about all of this before it's too late? We are certainly not the only country violating our earth. There are several other industrial nations guilty of fouling the air we breathe and the water we drink.

It isn't that we're not concerned. Our government has already passed much legislation intended to clean up our environment. Laws now provide for fines and even imprisonment in some cases to those who are guilty. But winning the battle is expensive and can sometimes lead to other less than pleasant implications. After considering all the implications of this very serious issue, write down your suggestions for dealing with the problem. Remember, it's your problem, too! You live in this great democracy where the people actively participate in the decisions that govern their lives. What plans do you have?

Name ____________________

THE HIGH COST OF HEALTH CARE

Rising costs for medicine and professional health services have created a new dilemma for the United States. Research has brought many revolutionary lifesaving and life-extending devices and techniques to the medical profession. While they make our lives better, they are not without their cost. The research behind them as well as the highly technical nature of most has placed them beyond the reach of many Americans they could serve. They have in fact almost created a society in which good health care is a luxury few can afford.

Medicare and Medicaid are government-sponsored programs designed to provide health care for the poor and the elderly, but they often fall short on extending the full range of health care available in medicine today. Just how does the government go about providing adequate health care for all its citizens? One answer would be for the government to control prices charged by doctors and other health care personnel. This is done in several other countries. There are, however, some implications in this plan.

In a society as large as ours, allowing the government to control pricing would go against the grain of the capitalistic spirit upon which this country was founded. What other problems do you see in allowing the government to provide some kind of national health plan? What do you think such a plan would do to the number of doctors our medical schools are producing each year?

____

____

____

____

____

____

Today good health care often comes down to a matter of whether the patient can afford to pay. This sometimes involves the transplant of life-giving organs. Those who can put the money up front get the care; those who cannot are denied. Is this right? What should the criteria be in determining who gets full health care services?

____

____

____

____

____

____

Name ______________________

VOTING REFORM

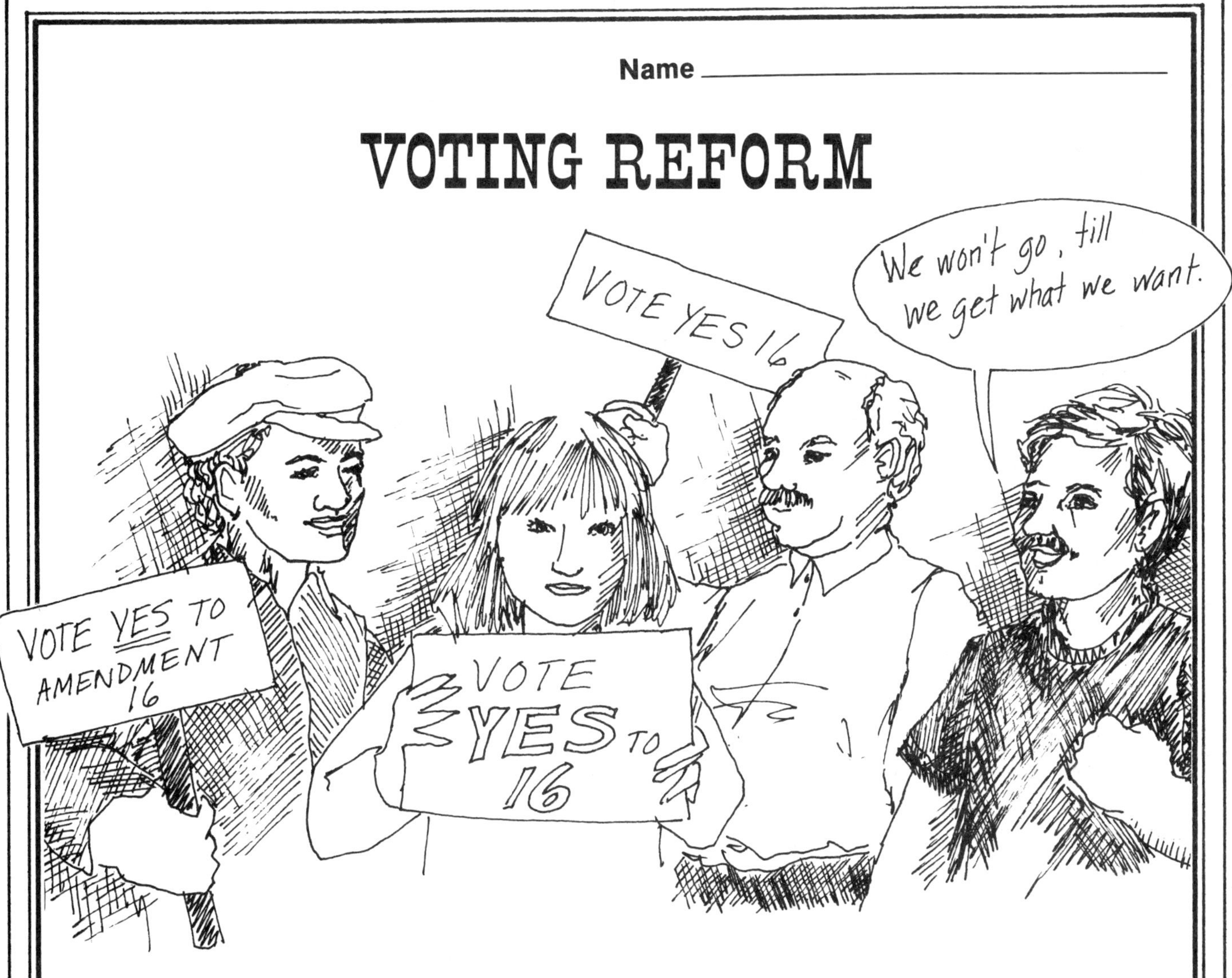

When the colonists first came to this land, they had rules on the right to vote that could cause one to seriously question calling the young nation a democracy. Being able to vote as we know it today didn't just happen overnight. The battle was long and difficult and involved lobby, protest, a lot of hard work and even violence on occasion. Most of the reforms were so important that they required changes to the Constitution. Research the text of the constitutional amendments listed below. Then match each amendment to the segment of the population affected by that amendment.

1. ____ 18-year-olds
2. ____ poor people who could not pay a poll tax
3. ____ women
4. ____ citizens of Washington, D.C.
5. ____ 21-year-old males who did not own property
6. ____ black males over 21 years of age

A. 14th Amendment
B. 15th Amendment
C. 19th Amendment
D. 23rd Amendment
E. 24th Amendment
F. 26th Amendment

SOCIAL REFORM

One of the biggest problems of living in a democracy is the failure on the part of the government to become actively involved in promoting social reform. By our earlier definitions, the more active the role of the government, the further removed we become from democracy in the true sense of the word. But there are certain programs and goals that are so large in size and scope that governmental involvement is almost a necessity to ensure their proper implementation.

A big difference between the political philosophies of the Democratic and Republican parties concerns the matter of social change. The Republican philosophy pushes for such decisions to be accomplished by volunteer organizations and local community action. On the other hand, Democrats lean toward favoring more active participation on the part of the federal government.

DISCRIMINATION

Even though the United States was founded on the principles of the true democracy, it has a long history of discrimination against minorities. Dating back to its beginnings when Blacks were used as slaves and continuing into the inner-city racial problems of today, it is quite clear that this country suffers from social inequality. Much has been done in the way of legislation, but much remains to achieve equality. Women in this country have also suffered discrimination in the past in the way of voting rights and more recently in job restrictions and equal pay. Just making all things equal isn't always the answer either. Look back at the problems caused by bussing in the 1970's. As long as there is as much prejudice as there is now and has been, there will be social inequalities.

Name ____________________

SOCIAL REFORM

List all the social injustices you can think of that cause certain group members in our society to live under conditions less fair than the American mainstream.

Where are the answers? What can be done to improve the lives of those being discriminated against? Is progress being made to achieve social equality?

Prejudice lies at the very heart of most discrimination against minorities. What can be done to reduce and eventually eliminate the prejudice in Americans that has led to the social injustices we still see in our society today?

What do you see as the most serious need for social reform in America today? Cite reasons for your choice and suggest ways to overcome the injustice.

TERRORISM

International terrorism continues to be a problem for the United States and other free countries around the world. Dealing with the demands of the terrorists presents one part of the dilemma. Handling the families and friends of the innocent victims provides the other. Such delicate matters require sensitive diplomacy and calm thinking.

The methods used by the terrorists vary, but often they involve the hijacking of planes filled with innocent hostages or the takeover of an entire building. Most terrorists use such tactics to gain an immediate forum of media coverage through which they can issue their demands and try to win supporters to their cause. Kidnapping dignitaries, starting fires, using time bombs, and open attacks on private citizens are other means by which terrorists gain public attention.

To this point the United States' position has been firm in refusing to yield to the demands of the terrorists. Imposing stiff penalties (including the death penalty for certain offenses) and imposing tighter security measures have been the chief weapons used by the federal government. Former President Reagan even launched a bombing attack on Libya in retaliation for certain terrorist attacks against the United States. The plan stopped such attacks at least for awhile, but innocent people were hurt and the bombing was condemned by many nations around the world.

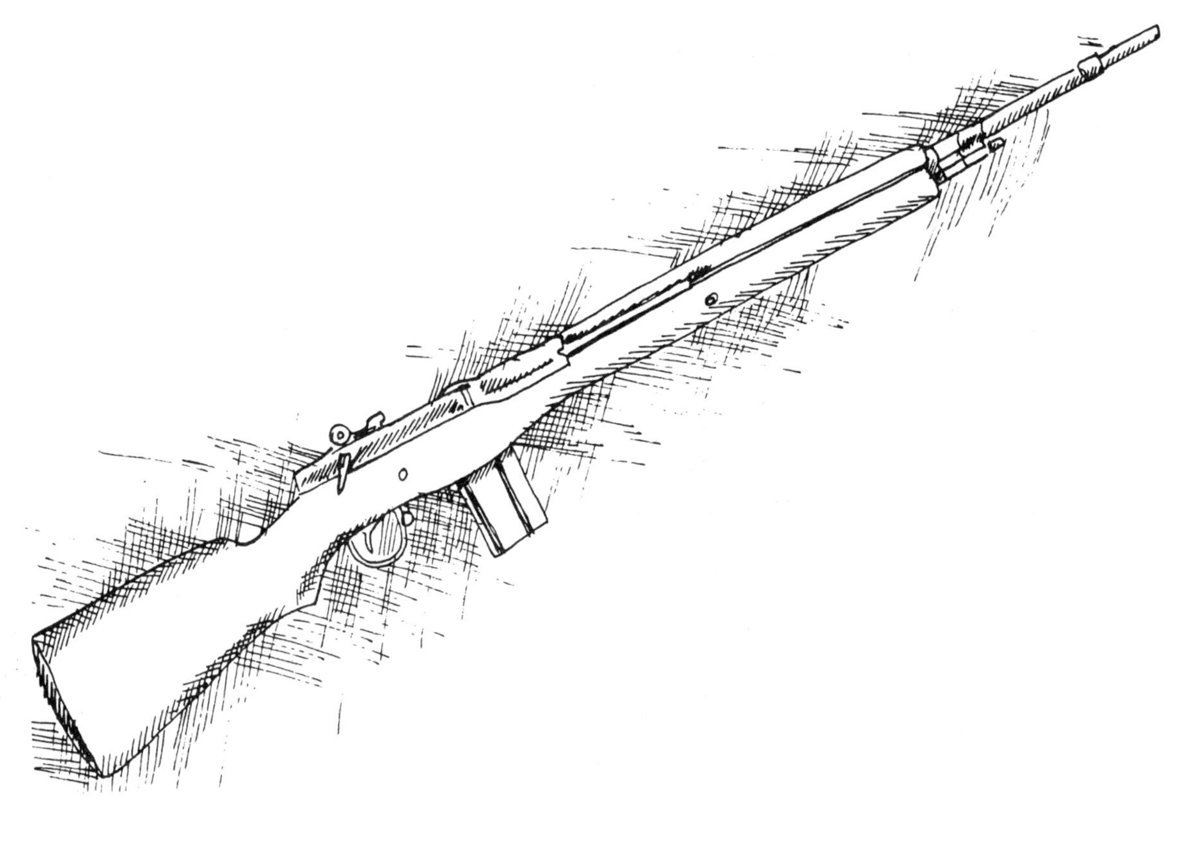

Name ______________________

TERRORISM

So the war on terrorism goes on. There may be a way to win such a war other than by the tactics currently being used. But at this point such terrorist acts continue to cause the citizens of this country to feel a little less secure and less certain than they would like to feel. What plan do you have for winning the U.S. war on terrorism?

Passengers boarding aircraft are currently required to pass through a security check that detects guns and other metal objects that might be used as weapons in a hijacking. All luggage passing through baggage goes through a similar check. While the number of hijack attempts in this country has decreased in the past few years, there are still enough to cause us concern. How do you explain why such attacks can still happen? What can be done to ensure that there will be no hijacking incidents whatsoever in the future? Would such measures be infringing on our personal right to privacy?

What should the penalty be for those who harm innocent U.S. citizens during terrorist attacks? What are the implications and problems involved when such attacks against U.S. citizens occur on foreign soil? What do you suggest the United States should do to ensure that the guilty are brought to justice?

Name ______________________

FOREIGN TRADE

The United States has long enjoyed the enviable position of having a foreign trade surplus; that is, we as a nation have exported more than we imported. That was good for us as a nation because it meant that goods produced in America were being sold all over the world. During the early 1980's, a dramatic change took place. Other countries began selling less expensive finished products to Americans. Sometimes the foreign-made goods were even superior in quality to the American-made products they were competing against. The result was that Americans began buying goods made abroad rather than those produced in the United States. Those same foreign products were also outselling American-made products in other countries, making it even more difficult to maintain a favorable balance of trade. Add to that the fact that agricultural technology has improved in other parts of the world, making those countries less dependent upon the American farmer. As a result of these changes, the United States now has a foreign trade deficit. Domestic businesses are struggling to survive. We as a nation are importing more than we export.

There are some potential solutions to the problem, but each one has some potentially negative implications. One of the problems of living in a democracy is the fact that solutions to problems must emerge through the voice and actions of the people. The answers are never simply dictated. To make it work, the people must get involved and make rational decisions based on research and good common sense.

Study the current foreign policy dilemma the United States is experiencing and present the alternatives to solving the problems. Discuss the negative consequences that accompany each. Then summarize your own position and decide how you suggest we solve the problems.

Name ______________________

DEMOCRACY IN ACTION

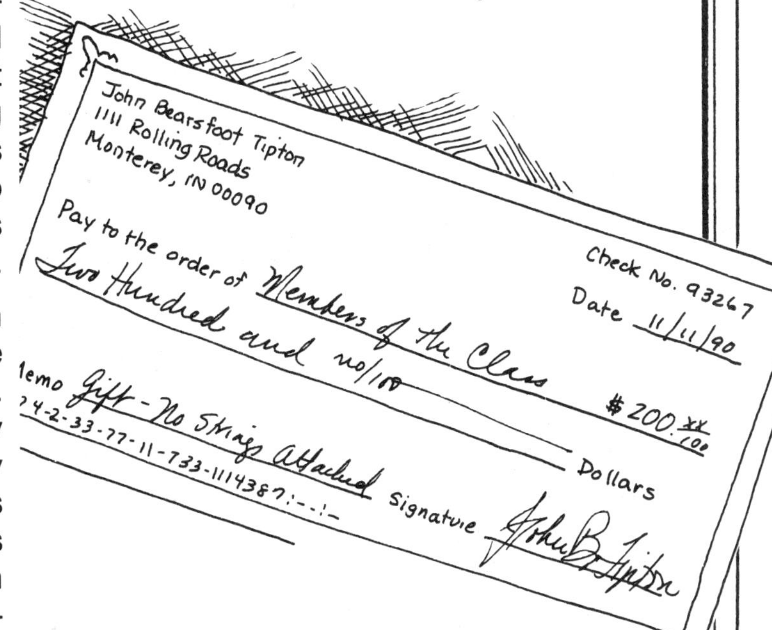

While the idea of democratic government may sound like an easy and natural way of life, we all know that getting people to agree on anything is usually a difficult, if not sometimes impossible, chore. To demonstrate to your class some of the difficulties involved, try the following simulation.

Members of the class have just been given $200.00. Never mind how it came to them. There are no strings attached. Children must decide democratically what to do with the money. The only ground rules are that the class is divided evenly into five groups. This is done by simply numbering children as they are seated. Each group is responsible for selecting one voting representative from among them. The method they use to determine who their representative will be can be of their own choosing. But it is the elected representatives who will make the final determination on what will be done with the money. All group members will provide suggestions to their representative on what to do with the money. The elected representatives will then meet to discuss alternatives. Once that group has narrowed down the possibilities, representatives return to their respective groups and discuss with their "people" the choices.

From that point, the representatives meet once again to make the final decision. Whatever the outcome, representatives return once again to their own reactions to that choice.

To get children started and to let them know there are no restrictions, provide a few initial suggestions. (For example, have a party, give the money to the Heart Fund, etc.) Discussion should follow at the conclusion of the simulation, paralleling the mechanics of our own government and the difficulties that are sometimes involved.

Name________________________________

FREEDOM FROM IGNORANCE

Thomas Jefferson once said:
"If a nation expects to be ignorant and free. . . it expects what never was and never will be."

What did Jefferson mean by that statement? That there is a responsibility placed upon the people who live in a democracy to stay abreast on the issues of the day. If they do not, that society will be controlled by people who have the power to make the decisions. But in all likelihood, those decisions won't be very good ones. It would be impossible to create and maintain a society that would then truly work.

Although Jefferson was a part of the aristocratic echelon of society, he nonetheless believed in rule by the people. But he wanted those people to be informed. Entering into each day armed with an adequate body of knowledge of the affairs of the day requires a certain amount of effort.

So we ask ourselves: "What all is involved in this responsibility we have to be properly informed?" On the key below, jot down some of the specific kinds of knowledge you feel we should all have to be acknowledged as *informed citizens* in this great democratic society in which we live.

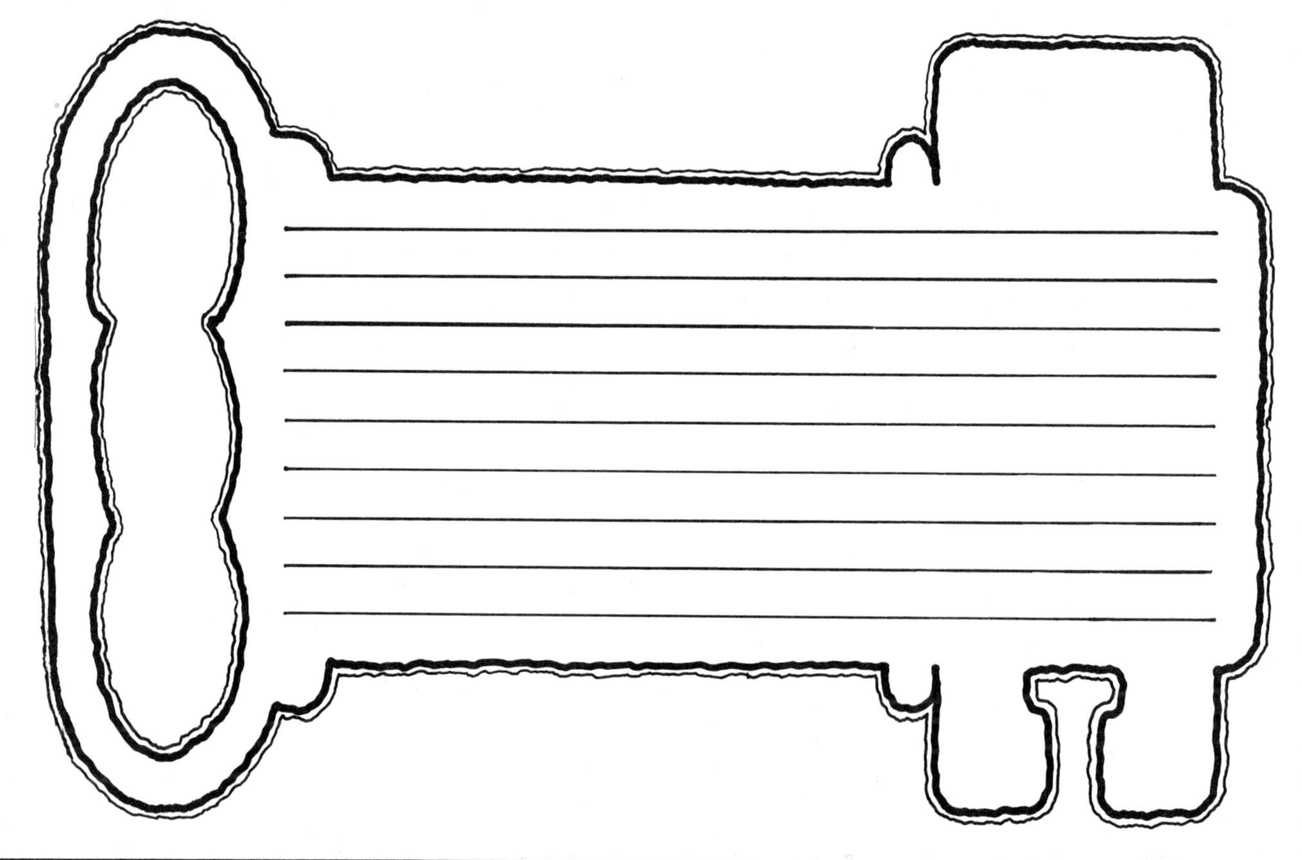

Name ____________________

WHY DEMOCRACY?

One of the biggest criticisms of a democracy is that it's an inefficient way to run a business, and it goes without saying that government is about the biggest business one can think of! Among the criticisms cited are these: It allows for a great deal of waste; there are people working in jobs which they know very little about. Money is often spent on programs without explanation or justification for where it will be coming from. And certainly allowing a single person or even a small group to make all the important decisions would ensure that such decisions are made as opposed to allowing the people to decide. Our democratic system of doing things often leads to procrastination and a lack of reaching an end result. Perhaps the biggest criticism of all, however, is that the "majority rules" philosophy doesn't always generate the most efficient and ready-made solutions to our problems.

It's almost as if we sometimes try to wish our problems away. In light of all these criticisms, we must ask ourselves the question why? Why do we tolerate such a system? If there are so many complaints against it, why don't we just "vote it out of office" as we do so many other ideas and people? Explain your own answers to these questions. Despite all the criticism that is constantly hurled at our system, we all know that democracy beats all other forms of government. Why? Because it includes us! We the people are involved. It not only includes us—it's for us! Reflect on these statements and explain what it is that makes democracy the best way to live and why we are so grateful to be a part of it.

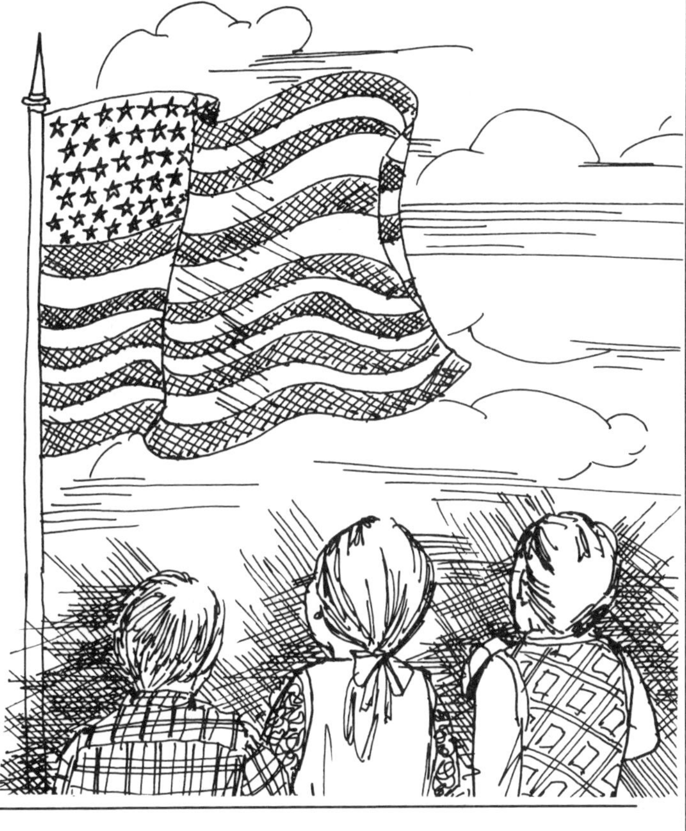

OPPONENTS OF DEMOCRACY

Several arguments have been advanced to point out the defects of democracy. In doing so, those who speak out against it usually follow up with an argument in support of an authoritarian system. While those people have the right to state their opinions, it's fairly easy to find flaws in their thinking. It really comes down to a case of what system we really support. For those of us who live in the free world and believe in democracy, the basic principle upon which we rest our case is that there are certain rights to which all men are entitled.

On the next page are some statements made by people who talk against democracy. Read each paragraph carefully. Then point out the flaws in their thinking that make the statements invalid to those of us who live in a democracy. We know we have the best system on Earth. Sometimes it requires a little thinking on our part to see the flaws in their ideas.

Name ____________________

OPPONENTS OF DEMOCRACY

Too much emphasis is placed on the natural inequality of man. Because there are wide differences in the skills, the intelligence and the natural ability of men, allowing each person the same voice in voting provides an avenue for the candidate with the ability to attract the most votes to win, even though most of the voters who elected the candidate may be inferior members of society.

Democratic governments are effective and oftentimes corrupt. Selfish deals are made behind closed doors at the expense of the general welfare of the people. Many of the legislators who are supposedly representing all the people find themselves committed to special interest groups.

Many of the "elected few" are only interested in satisfying their own desires. They show little regard for the public welfare, becoming more overly involved in the task of lining their own pockets. Unsavory politicians see the spoils of their office as a way to line their own pockets.

A society emphasizing equality leads to demands for equality that are detrimental to both that society and individual members. Personal liberties in the accumulation of wealth and getting good leaders as officeholders are often sacrificed because of the philosophy that everyone should be equal. Democracy calls for the elimination of these inequalities that help to make a country great.

In a democracy the public is suspicious of change. As a result, important reforms and needed legislation are often postponed. Politicians do not want to jeopardize their position with the voting public, especially during an election year. Educating the public is difficult because of the prejudice and ignorance of many people. As a result it is very difficult to get things done. People are content with the way things are. Democracy bogs down the wheels of progress.

Name ______________________________

IN THE YEAR 2020

We live in an ever-changing world. Since the people of the United States participate (either directly or indirectly) in the decisions of its government and society, the people must be willing to help in solving the problems that continually emerge. By the time the year 2020 arrives, there will have been a great many changes that will have taken place. We will have new priorities and new problems to deal with. Since we are involved in the affairs of our government, we must also be willing to help find answers to its problems. Certain concerns about our future have already been expressed by those who are looking ahead.

One of our major responsibilities in inhabiting this earth is to pass it on to later generations in no worse condition than it was when we inherited it from our forefathers. Some people are concerned today about our inability to do that. They say we're destroying the ozone layer and that we are actually changing the climate of the earth through our reckless living and life-style that keeps us in the "comfort zone."

What will be our major concerns in the year 2020? Time and technology will change the way we live. Discuss what you feel will be our chief problems and concerns and offer suggestions on how they should be dealt with by this democratic society.

____

____

____

____

____

____

____

____

____

Name ____________________

100 REASONS WHY I LOVE AMERICA. . .

Sometimes we hear so much from those who complain about America that we lose sight of how great it really is. . . and how fortunate we are to live here! There are, after all, few countries on Earth where the essentials of democracy are so available to us all. So let's start counting the reasons. You need not use complete sentences, but start numbering and list as many reasons as you can. If you really think about all the many freedoms and blessings you enjoy in this country, it won't be hard to reach 100. If you really get going, why stop at a hundred? You will need additional paper.

Name ______________________

WHAT PRICE WE PAY?

One of the pleasures of living in a democracy is the freedom to pursue whatever career or occupation we desire. That choice must someday be made by each of us. There are several factors and priorities that enter into the final decision. Money is usually a main consideration, but location, job security, hours worked, education required, and type of work may also enter into the eventual choice we make.

Let's start with money. Below are some occupations in one column and an equal number of annual salaries in the other column. Your task is to match them up according to your own priorities based on the value to our society each provides.

	Occupation	Salary
______	Minister	a. $37,000
______	Small Business Owner	b. $60,000
______	Lawyer	c. $35,000
______	Factory Worker	d. $100,000
______	Nurse	e. $9500
______	Automobile Salesman	f. $72,000
______	Surgeon	g. $250,000
______	Judge	h. $28,000
______	Major League Baseball Star	i. $43,000
______	Elementary School Teacher	j. $300,000
______	President	k. $22,000
______	Car Wash Attendant	l. $400,000
______	Sales Clerk in a Department Store	m. $1,000,000
______	Chairman of the Board at General Motors	n. $16,000
______	Movie Star	o. $3,000,000
______	Commercial Fisherman	p. $38,500

Did you rank order the salaries according to the way you think the distribution should be or the way you think they are ranked in the real world? Explain your choice for the $3,000,000 "top job."

____

____

____

Name ____________________

WHAT PRICE WE PAY?

Location is another factor to consider when looking for a life's work. Rank your choices below beginning with your favorite choice as #1.

____ Rural New England
____ Chicago
____ Rural Kansas
____ Northern California
____ Albuquerque, New Mexico
____ Oklahoma
____ Phoenix, Arizona
____ Washington, D.C.
____ Portland, Oregon
____ Minneapolis, Minnesota
____ Juneau, Alaska
____ The Florida Keys
____ New Orleans, Louisiana
____ Boston, Massachusetts
____ New York City
____ San Diego, California
____ Other ____________

When it comes to education, place a check mark (✓) beside all which you intend to complete.

____ Elementary School
____ High School
____ Junior College
____ Four-Year College
____ Advanced Degree
____ Other ____________

Considering the above factors and those mentioned on the preceding page of this activity, decide which seems most important to you at this point in your life. Rank order the following according to your own preference:

____ Money
____ Education
____ Hours Worked
____ Location
____ Job Security
____ Type of Work Done

Explain your choice of that which seems most important to you.

____
____
____
____

Name ____________________

WHAT CAN I DO?

Ralph Nader, one of America's most famous "private citizens," once said, "There can be no daily democracy without daily citizenship. If we do not exercise our civic rights, who will? If we do not perform our civic duties, who can? The fiber of a just society in pursuit of happiness is a thinking active citizenry. That means you.

Probably one of the first things you think about when you hear someone talking about being a good public citizen is exercising the right to vote. But you are too young to vote. So what can you do? For one thing, you can obey all the laws that have been made by the lawmakers we elect to office. You might also write letters to your lawmakers expressing your views on public issues. And to have a view on such matters, you should read newspapers and magazines and watch or listen to news reports that will make you informed on matters that concern us all.

But there are several other things you can do, too, to become more actively involved in this democracy of which you are a part. In the space below list at least ten additional ideas you have which you yourself can do to be termed a *good citizen.*

Name ____________________

GOOD CITIZEN AWARD

Reproduce a Good Citizen Award for each student in your class. Suggest that each child think privately about whom he or she should nominate for best citizen. This person can be a classmate, the student himself, a person within the community, or even someone of national or world renown. Emphasis should be placed on justifying whatever choice the student makes. Nominations are made for those who actively participate in our government by obeying the laws and helping whenever possible to support the democratic ideals under which we live.

Good Citizen Award
The Most Honorable

The Most Honorable ________________ is hereby nominated to receive the Good Citizen Award for the following reasons:

____

____

____

____

____

____

____

____

Date ________________ Signed ____________________

A FINAL WORD

The dynamic, rapidly changing world in which we live places us on the threshold of perhaps the greatest period of human evolution ever. Research and technology have placed endless opportunities before us, but there are also dangers involved. Transportation and communication advances have placed other nations at our doorstep. But so have the vast storehouses of nuclear armaments owned by many nations on our earth. We can no longer live in isolation for our own concerns and those of the people of the United States. We have an obligation to cooperate and learn to cohabit peacefully with even those nations we don't consider friendly to us.

We must do this to save our resources, to save ourselves and to save our earth for future generations. Our leaders must have the thought and foresight to continually progress toward this goal. There is no place for irrational selfish thoughts and actions. We must think together and we must act together if we are to preserve our earth for those who will come after us.

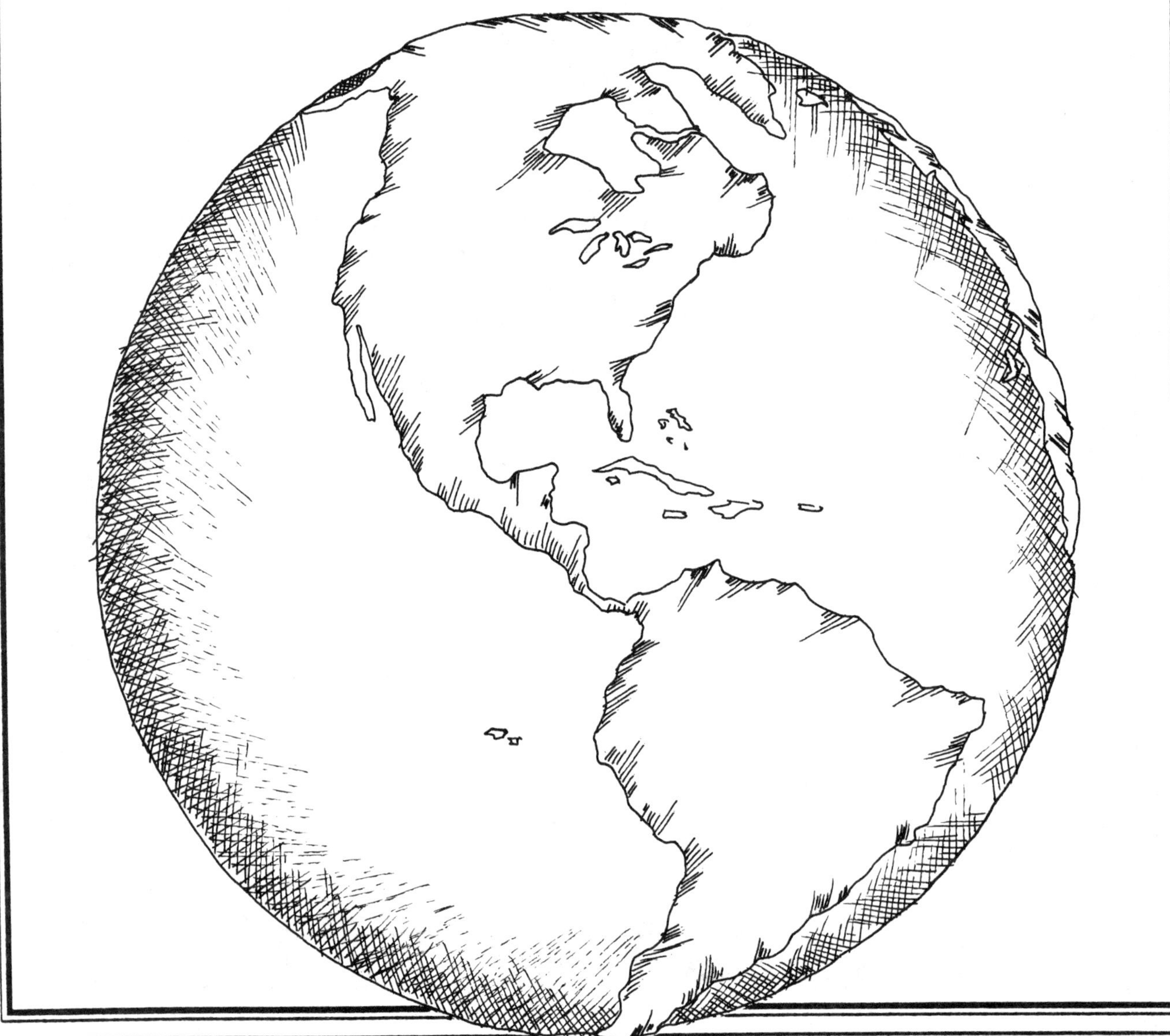

Name ______________________

A FINAL WORD

The statements below are those made by Americans who have a strong hope for our future and feel there is a definite direction in which we should be directing our energies. Look at each statement carefully. Then decide which you think offers the best hope for us and future generations. Place a #1 beside that statement. Then rank order the other four statements according to your priority. The statement with a 5 beside it should be the statement you feel is least important.

____ We should address ourselves to solving the problems of the ugliness and sickness caused by our polluted air, land and water.

____ We should be pushing for all nations on Earth to live democratically. If they did, the world would be a better place.

____ Our most important goal should be to make the whole world free from the threats of nuclear war. Once that is accomplished, we will be able to do many other things.

____ If we could solve the problems of hunger and starvation around the world, we would be along the road toward making our earth a better place to live.

____ Prejudice and hatred are at the very root of most of the problems we have, not only in this country but around the rest of the world as well. If we could only eliminate such ugliness, then there is still hope for us.

Defend your favorite choice and explain your position on why you feel the choice you made does indeed provide real hope for the United States and the rest of the world.

PROJECTS FOR EXTENDED STUDY

Assign or modify any of the topics below for further research and development.

Democracy—Myth or Reality

The Real Meaning of Democracy

The Role of the People in a Democracy

Leadership in a Democracy

Criterion for a Modern Democracy

Voting in a Democracy

Capitalism Vs. Socialism

Capitalism Vs. Communism

Majority Rule

Democracy over Authoritarianism

Today's Democracy

The Essentials of Liberty

"Socialized" Democracy

Various Meanings of *Democracy*

Restrictions in a Democracy

The Need for Rules in a Democracy

Freedom of Religion in a Democracy

Democracy in America

Examples of Democracy at Work

Representation in a Democracy

Freedom of Speech: An Essential of Democracy

Democracy in Its Pure State No Longer Exists

Party Politics

Free Enterprise: Where Competition Is King

The Role of the Young Citizen in a Democracy

Obligations of Living in a Democracy

ANSWER KEY

LINCOLN'S DEMOCRACY Page 9

1. He did not want to alienate those slave states that had remained loyal to the Union.
2. Answers will vary.
3. Answers will vary.

CAPITALISM, SOCIALISM AND COMMUNISM Pages 12-13

1. Capitalism
2. Communism
3. Socialism
4. Socialism
5. Capitalism
6. Communism
7. Capitalism
8. Socialism
9. Capitalism
10. Socialism
11. Communism
12. Communism
13. Capitalism
14. Socialism
15. Socialism or Capitalism
16. Capitalism
17. Socialism
18. Socialism
19. Communism
20. Capitalism

CHOOSING OUR LEADERS Page 15

1. Answers will vary.
2. Answers will vary.
3. An obligation to become informed on the issues in question and the practices of those who are running on those issues.

ELECTING OUR PRESIDENT Pages 17-19

1. CA, NY, OH, TX, PA, IL, FL, MI
2. The number of electoral votes is insignificant when compared to the larger states.
3. If two candidates are vying for the presidency, the candidate who loses will no doubt be embittered and be less than supportive of the President's policies. Also, under the system today, the politics of the winning party usually prevail.
4. Answers will vary but should include either a split among the electors (according to the people) or abandoning the Electoral College altogether in favor of a popular vote of the people.
5. 1824—John Quincy Adams, Andrew Jackson, William H. Crawford, Henry Clay
   1876—Rutherford B. Hayes, Samuel J. Tilden
   1888—Benjamin Harrison, Grover Cleveland

THE ELECTORAL DISTRIBUTION Page 20

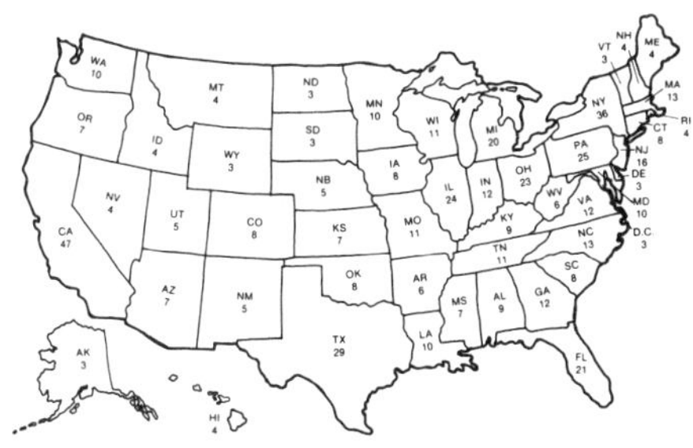

ELECTION DAY Pages 22-23

1. They felt most of the people lacked proper knowledge to make wise decisions, and they were afraid residents of populous states would band together and elect whatever candidate they chose.
2. Each state was allowed a number of electors equal to the number of senators and representatives it had in Congress.
3. Each party now runs a presidential candidate *and* a candidate for Vice President. A winning team is elected rather than having the winner be President and the runner-up Vice President.
4. The presidential candidates are normally from different parties; hence their political views would not be the same. This would make it difficult for them to work together. There would also be some natural resentment on the part of the Vice President as he was the loser in the presidential race, and probably some feelings of ill will.
5. Each state could appoint electors in any manner it chose. Today they are chosen by the political parties.
6. The election of the President is sent to the House of Representatives where each state gets one vote.

THE ELECTORAL COLLEGE TODAY Page 25

1. Answers will vary but should include statement against "winner-take-all" philosophy where a candidate with fewer popular votes can win the presidency.
2. a. If the "minority" candidate were to win the big states by a slim margin, then lost the states with fewer electors by a large margin, it would be possible for a candidate with fewer popular votes from the people to become President.
   b. If there was a strong third party candidate running who gained enough votes to prevent either of the major candidates from winning a majority of electors, the election would be thrown into the House of Representatives.
3. Answers will vary.

CONSERVATISM VS. LIBERALISM VS. REPUBLICANISM Page 27

1. C
2. C
3. L
4. L
5. R
6. L
7. R
8. R
9. C
10. C
11. R
12. R
13. C
14. L
15. C
16. R
17. C
18. L
19. C
20. R

SENSITIVE ISSUES Page 34

Arizona—Illegal Aliens
Iowa—Farm Prices
Arkansas—Equal Rights
Louisiana—Offshore Oil Rights
Michigan—Water Pollution
Maine—Fishing Rights

ELECTION TRIVIA Page 37

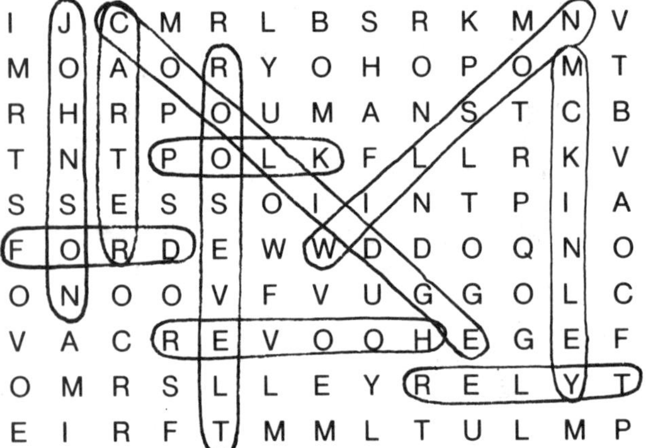

POLL WATCHING Page 38

1. A
2. 22%
3. 10%
4. Probably emphasize this candidate's lead and perhaps devote energy toward gaining undecided vote.

ELECTIONS OF THE PAST Page 42

1. 1824
2. John Adams
3. 1800
4. Lyndon Johnson
5. John Quincy Adams
6. 1960
7. Thomas Jefferson
8. 33
9. Franklin D. Roosevelt
10. 35
11. Grover Cleveland
12. Thomas Jefferson
13. John Quincy Adams
14. 3—1824, 1876, 1888
15. 1960
16. Ronald Reagan, 525
17. Franklin D. Roosevelt, election of 1936—523-8
18. 69
19. Dwight D. Eisenhower
20. William H. Harrison
21. Alfred Landon 8, 1936
22. Martin Van Buren
23. 14
24. 401
25. He was 18.4% (or 99 electoral votes) closer than Mondale.

THE RIGHT OF DISSENT Pages 45-46

1. . . .That what is vulgar to one person might well be a part of another's normal vocabulary. . .and to say who is right is a part of censorship which the court was trying to disallow.
2. If the deed can be construed to provoke others to violence or disturbance; then it can be restricted.

RIGHTS OF THE ACCUSED Page 55

1. To even bring the accused before the court required first a formal indictment by a grand jury. The grand jury will hear the evidence against Kelly and in this case (because of her alibi) probably drop the charge.
2. The double jeopardy clause forbids trying the accused a second time on the same offense.
3. The accused cannot be forced to bear witness against himself. The burden of proving a defendant guilty rests on the prosecution.

BARDEE'S QUIK STOP Pages 56-57

1. The court will appoint a qualified attorney to represent him in court.
2. He can subpoena Marshall into court and force him to testify under oath.
3. He can force her to testify in court under oath and the threat of perjury if her story proves to be untrue. She will also be questioned by Billy's attorney.
4. Answers will vary but should reflect the rights of the accused under the Sixth Amendment.
   a. Must be properly informed of the nature of the charge.
   b. Has the right to confront face-to-face those who testify against him.
   c. Has the right to subpoena witnesses in his behalf.
   d. Has the right to an attorney even if he has no money.
   e. The right to a speedy trial.

FINIAS BUTCHER'S LAND Pages 59-60

1. The government does indeed have the right to take the land of private individuals if it is determined that taking that land is in the best interest of all.
2. He can fight the battle in court citing his reasons why the government should not take his land.
3. Answers will vary. He should try to fight the matter in court, and if he loses the ability to keep his property, he should file a suit to get a much more equitable price.
4. Answers will vary.
5. Answers will vary.

LOCAL LAWS Pages 66-67

1. There are situations where the best interest of the people in a certain area can best be served by making laws that apply directly to a specific condition of living.
2. Size of community, location, education of residents, type of community, etc. Accept other answers.
6. At the local level there is a closer participation by the people themselves into the actual lawmaking process.

EXECUTIVE ORDER 9066 Page 76

2. 1850's—California Gold Rush
   1860's—Workers needed for construction of Central Pacific Railroad

VOTING REFORM Page 87

1. F
2. E
3. C
4. D
5. A
6. B